My Feelings, My Self

Revised edition of *Lynda Madaras' Growing-Up Guide for Girls*

LYNDA MADARAS
with AREA MADARAS

Drawings by Jackie Aher

Newmarket Press   New York

Revised edition of *Lynda Madaras Growing-Up Guide for Girls,* originally published in 1986.

Copyright © 1993 Lynda Madaras

This book published simultaneously in the United States of America and in Canada.

93 94 95   10 9 8 7 6 5 4 3 2 1

Library of Congress Cataloging-in-Publication Data

Madaras, Lynda
     My feelings, my self: Lynda Madaras' growing-up guide for girls/Lynda Madaras with Area Madaras.
                    p.   cm.
     Includes bibliographical references and index.
     Summary: The authors use text, quizzes, exercises, and letters to present information about relationships with parents and friends, self-awareness, peer pressure, and other concerns of teenage girls.
     ISBN 1-55704-157-1
     1. Teenage girls—Psychology—Problems, exercises, etc.—Juvenile literature. 2. Adolescent psychology—Problems, exercises, etc.—Juvenile literature. [1. Teenage girls.] I. Madaras, Area. II. Title.
HQ798.M2933 1993
305.23'5-dc20   *93-9877*
                                                              CIP
                                                              AC

Quantity purchases:
Companies, professional groups, clubs, and other organizations may qualify for special terms when ordering quantities of this title. For information write Special Sales, Newmarket Press, 18 East 48th Street, New York, NY 10017, or call (212) 832-3575.

Drawings by Jackie Aher

Manufactured in the United States of America

CONTENTS

INTRODUCTION: YOUR GROWING-UP YEARS

Most books are written *about* other people, and they are usually written *by* other people.

This book is a little different. It's about *you*, and *you* will be doing a lot of the writing.

This book is a combination workbook/journal/diary. It's filled with quizzes, interviews, and exercises for you to do. And, at certain places in this book, you'll have a chance to write about your own thoughts and feelings or about what's happening in your life. If the book is yours, it's okay to write in it, but if it belongs to your library you may want to use tracing paper for the quizzes, and get a workbook to start your own journal.

Since this book is about you, let's start with you:

My name is _____.

Today's date is _____.

I am _____ years and _____ months old.

I am _____ feet and _____ inches tall.

I weigh _____ pounds.

This book is about your growing-up years, about your preteen and teen years — the years when your body is changing from a child's body into a woman's body.

This time of changing is called *puberty*. Another name for these years is *adolescence.*

During puberty, your body changes in many ways. But it's not just your body that changes during these years. Your whole life changes! You make new friends. You try new things. You start to depend on your parents less and to become more independent. You start to have more of a say in making the decisions that affect your life. Best friends or being part of a certain gang or group may become more important than ever before. You may develop crushes. You may begin to have romantic feelings about a certain special someone. You may start dating or "going with" someone.

These changes and the other changes that take place in your life during adolescence can be very exciting. They can also be a bit (or a lot!) scary or confusing at times. It isn't always easy to deal with all these changes. This book will talk about some of these life changes, and we hope it will help you handle these changes a little more smoothly.

"We" are Lynda and Area Madaras, the mother/daughter team who put this book together. Lynda (the mom) is a writer who teaches classes in sex education and adolescence to preteen and teenage girls and boys. Area (the daughter) was a sixteen-year-old high school senior when this book was first written. She is now a graduate student at USC. A few years ago, the two of us wrote a book together called *The "What's Happening to My Body?" Book for Girls,* in which we explained the physical changes that happen in a girl's body during puberty.*

We are happy to say that lots and lots of mothers and daughters bought and read our first book. Many of them were kind enough to write and tell us how much they enjoyed the book (which made us feel real proud of ourselves!). Many of the girls who wrote to us also asked us to answer questions they had, not only about the body changes of puberty, but about how to get along with their parents, about boyfriends, dating, best friends, peer pressure, and their own feelings about the changes that were happening in their lives.

We received so many letters from girls that we started thinking it might be a good idea to do another book that would talk not just about the physical, body changes of puberty, but about some of the other changes that take place in a girl's life during her growing-up years. Our publisher, Esther Margolis, thought it might be more interesting if we did something a little different this time. She suggested that we make this a book where girls would actually do things instead of just

---

puberty (PEW-bur-tee) Throughout this book there may be words that you don't know how to pronounce, so we've included a pronunciation key like this at the bottom of the page whenever there's a word that you may have trouble pronouncing. *The capital letters indicate the part of the word that is stressed when it is pronounced.*

adolescence (ad-a-LESS-ence)

*Later on, Lynda and a boy student Dane Saavedra wrote a similar book on male puberty called *The "What's Happening to My Body?" Book for Boys.*

reading the book. And that's how we came up with the idea of doing *Lynda Madaras' Growing-Up Guide for Girls* which we published in 1986. This book was a combination journal/diary in which girls could write about their own lives, and also a workbook with lots of fun quizzes and exercises.

During the next few years, we got even more mail from girls with even more questions, some about body changes, others about boys, parents, and friends. So, when 1993 rolled around and my publisher suggested doing another book, we all realized that we had enough material not for one book, but for two. We wanted to do one just on the body changes, and another in which girls could explore their feelings about growing up so we wrote *My Body, My Self* and *My Feelings, My Self.*

My Body, My Self is the workbook companion to *The "What's Happening to My Body?" Book for Girls* and includes over 100 quizzes, checklists, journal entries and exercises to help girls address their questions and concerns about their changing bodies. *My Feelings, My Self* focuses on relationships, feelings, self-knowledge, problem-solving with parents, handling peer pressure, and making friends.

USING THIS BOOK

As you'll discover, this book is divided into three parts.

The first part of the book, "Your Friends," talks about things like popularity, peer pressure, making friends, best friends, crushes, and the opposite sex.

Part Two, "Your Parents," talks about how and why your relationship with your parents changes during adolescence. It also includes some exercises that can help you to communicate better with your parents and to find ways to solve some of the problems that your family may face during your growing-up years.

Last but not least, there's Part Three, which includes suggestions for further reading, and information on getting help for special problems.

As we say, we hope this book will help make your growing-up years a little easier and much more fun. We also hope you'll save this book so that you can come back to it again and again. (You might even want to hang on to this book even after you've become an adult. If someday you become the mother of a girl child, your daughter will no doubt get a big kick out of reading what you've written.)

Finally, there's one important way that this book is a little different from other books: You don't have to start at page one and go straight through to the end. You can hop, skip, and jump around according to what interests you most at this particular time in your life. You may find that you want to do certain sections now and do other sections later on.

If you do want to skip around, we should tell you that pages in Part Two contain some quizzes, information, and exercises that are in a certain special order. Unless you've done the *first* quizzes and exercises in this section, you may not understand the later ones. So it's best to work through pages in order. Other than this, though, you can feel free to skip around in this book and to do things in any order that you feel like doing them.

Freewriting

Sometimes, to help you get started writing in this book, we'll include an exercise in something called freewriting. We first learned about freewriting from a book called *Writing as a Second Language*, by Barbara Danish. Freewriting is a way of getting around the hang-ups most of us have about writing. It's a way of getting over your fear of a blank page.

When you freewrite, you write without stopping. You don't have to rush, but you do write without stopping. You write whatever comes into your head. You put your pen or pencil to the page and just keep writing until you've filled up the entire page or pages. You don't have to worry about spelling or grammar or punctuation. You don't have to worry about what you're going to say next or whether what you're writing sounds logical or makes sense. You're free to write without worrying how it sounds or whether it's "right" or "good." You just write whatever pops into your mind. The only rule in freewriting is that you have to keep writing the whole time. Don't stop if you can help it. If you do stop, don't lift your pen or pencil from the paper. Don't go back and rewrite, or cross out, or correct. Try to keep writing. If you can't think of anything to write, just repeat the last word you've written over and over or write, "I can't think of anything to write," over and over until you do think of something.

If you find that you have trouble freewriting because you're worried about what someone else may think if they read it, remember that this is your private workbook/journal/diary. You don't have to show it to anyone else unless you want to. If you do find yourself getting stuck in your freewriting because you're worried about what someone else might think (or what you yourself might think when you read it later), just write that. Write, "I'm having trouble freewriting because I'm worried what it might sound like to someone else (or to me later on)." You could go on to say more about why you're worried or you could just keep writing the same sentence over and over. It doesn't matter. Just keep freewriting.

Below are examples of two people's first attempt at freewriting, to give you a better idea of how freewriting works (each of these people was writing for about two or three minutes).

"Well, here goes. She said just to keep writing and to write whatever comes into my head without stopping, but not to rush. Suddenly, there's nothing at all in my head and I feel like I have to rush. In fact I'm rushing so much that my hand is hurting from holding onto my pencil so hard and trying to write so fast. I guess I'll just make an effort to slow down and let my thoughts come out, but as soon as I think about that my mind goes blank blank blank blank.

That's funny isn't it. My writing so fast and rushing and then when I slow down I find that I don't have much to say and that gets me all uptight and makes me start to rush. I guess it's really scary in some ways not to know what to say and to find out there's not very much going on in my head. I guess writing my thoughts is kind of scary (stop)."

"I sometimes wonder why we are here, and what is our purpose. It's kind of like a story and on one hand, we'd like to know why we're here and how the story will end, but on the other hand, we are afraid to find out. I guess that fear is basically a fear of death but I'm not sure. It's possible that the fear is merely of the (stop.)"

Once you've had some practice at freewriting, you'll find that it gets easier and easier, and you won't be stuck writing things like, "I can't think of anything to write," as often.

You'll find freewriting exercises throughout this book. We put these freewriting execises in the book instead of just asking you to write in a regular way (like you were writing an essay for English class or writing in the usual sort of journal or diary) because we think it will work better for most of you.

If you've ever tried to keep a diary or a journal, you probably know what kinds of problems people run into. A lot of us sit down in front of that clean, white, blank diary or journal page, and we don't ever get around to writing anything because we don't want to "mess up." When you freewrite, you don't have to worry about sloppy writing, misspelled words, writing something that doesn't sound good or "messing up." You're supposed to mess up. That's the whole point of freewriting—to be free to write and to make mistakes, to mess up, or simply to write whatever pops into your mind. There's an old saying that sometimes we don't really know how we feel about something until we try to write it down. It's a *wise* old saying.

1 / YOUR FRIENDS

Just as our bodies and our relationships with our parents change during puberty and adolescence, so do our relationships with our friends and with the other kids we know. For one thing, as we become more independent from our parents, our friends usually come to play a larger role in our lives. In fact, many of the young people we talked to told us that they spent more time with and felt closer to their friends than to their own families at this point in their lives. This is a time when belonging to a certain group or crowd of friends and being liked and accepted by others may become more important to us than they ever were before. We may also start to get interested in the opposite sex. We may develop crushes, start liking a certain special someone, begin having boyfriends, or start dating.

These changes are the subject of this part of the book. We talked to lots of preteens and teens in order to write it. We also talked to grown-ups and asked them to tell us about their growing-up years. In the following sections we'll be letting you know what they had to say about friendship, best friends, popularity, peer pressure, crushes, boyfriends, dating, and other topics. We'll also be asking you to think and write about your own feelings, thoughts, and ideas.

1: BEST FRIENDS

Most of the preteen and teenage girls we interviewed told us that they had one or more best friends. Many girls said that their relationship with their best friend was one of the most important things (or *the most* important thing!) in their lives. Here's what some of the girls we talked to had to say about best friends:

We're like sisters, only better! We don't have to pretend or put on an act around each other. We can just be ourselves.

—Janelle, age 13

Your best friend is someone who understands you and who likes you regardless of rumors or what anyone else says. . . . You can get irate with her—totally mad—and still be friends. . . . You can talk about anything with your best friend.

—Shelly, age 14

You can just be silent. You don't always have to talk or explain everything. Your best friend just understands. You don't ever have to feel uncomfortable. You don't have to worry about losing her to other people. She's always your best friend.

—Beth, age 15

My best friend and I have been through a lot together. We've shared good times and also hard times. . . . Your best friend sticks by you, no matter what happens. A lot of times, if there's something rotten going on, other

people stay away or avoid you or act like they hardly ever even knew you.
Your best friend sticks around!

—Sophia, age 11

Some of the adult women we interviewed told us that they were still friends with the people they'd been best friends with during their growing-up years. Sometimes these friendships lasted even though the people involved had grown up, moved away from each other, and now lived thousands of miles apart. One woman told us:

I don't see Jane much anymore. She lives in Washington, D.C., and I
live on the west coast, but we've stayed in touch. When I'm back east or
she's out here, we always get together. Each time we see each other, it's
like all the years in between never even happened. We sit up all night talk-
ing and giggling like we did when we were thirteen.
And, she's still there when I need her—like, when my mom died, she
came out and helped me with the funeral and all. . . . She recently had
a baby and I'm the godmother . . .
We always laugh and say that even when we're grey-haired old ladies
sitting on our porches in our rocking chairs, we'll still be getting to-
gether and staying up all night giggling and talking just like thirteen-
year-olds.

Of course, not all the friends we have now will still be part of our lives when we're older. Even the best of friends drift apart and eventually lose touch with each other. But some friendships remain, despite the years and miles that may separate us.

One fourteen-year-old girl that we talked to had something interesting to say about lasting friendships:

Right now I have a boyfriend and I spend a lot of time with him. I
don't see so much of my best friend anymore because of spending so much
time with my boyfriend. My mom said something that made me think.
She said, "You know, romances and boyfriends come and go, but best
friends often stay. Chances are you won't even know or will hardly re-
member [your boyfriend] twenty years from now. But, if you don't ne-
glect your friendship with [your best friend], that's a friendship you
may have your whole life through."

Of course, not everyone has a best friend. Some people that we talked to who didn't have a best friend felt pretty bad about it. One girl said:

My family moved and I'm going to a new school. I don't know anybody.
I miss my best friend. I don't have anybody yet to take her place. It's so
lonely for me. I don't have anyone to talk to. I cry sometimes.

Although some people feel pretty lonely without a best friend, others don't feel quite as upset as this girl. For instance, another girl told us that she was "kind of a loner" and that she had hardly any friends, let alone a best friend. She said that she "kind-of wished" she did have one, so she'd have someone to share her "innermost thoughts" with. But she said that she spent a lot of time writing her thoughts and feelings in a journal she kept, and her writing helped her a lot. There were also some people who told us that they didn't have close friendships because so much of their time was taken up pursuing a career or a goal they'd set for themselves. For instance, one girl who was a violinist told us:

> *I've been studying violin since I was four, and I'm very serious about my music. I work with my teacher several afternoons a week and on Saturdays. At other times, I'm practicing—I rehearse for competitions—and it doesn't leave much time for anything else. I've made a commitment to this and it's my life, though I know in some ways I'm missing out on what normal teenagers do. I don't have close friends. I don't have a social life. I don't have a boyfriend. I don't have time for the normal things of growing up. . . . I'm always working, but I love it. It's worth it to me.*

By and large, though, the preteens and teens who didn't have a best friend felt that not having a close friend was a real lack in their lives. If you don't have a best friend, but would like to have one, be sure to read the section "Making Friends."

Your Best Friend

Most of the preteens and teens we talked to told us that they had one or two or more best friends. How about you? Do you have a best friend or friends? If so, we'd like you to draw a picture of your best friend in the space below. Don't worry if you're not the world's greatest artist. You can even draw a stick-figure thing—just so it gives some idea of what your friend looks like. (Or, if you're too chicken to draw, you could paste a photo of your friend in the space below.)

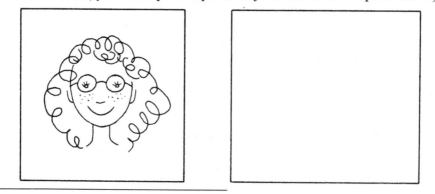

My friend.   Draw an outline, like the one at left, or paste a photo in the space.

EXERCISE

Now we'd like you to write about the friendship you two share by filling in the blank space below. If you have more than one best friend, pick one to write about. If you don't have a best friend right now, you might write about a best friend you've had in the past. Or, you might decide to wait until you do have a best friend before doing this exercise.

1. My best friend's is _____. She (or he) is _____ years old.

2. The way we first met and got to be friends was _____

_____

_____

_____

3. The main reason why the two of us are friends is _____

_____

_____

_____

_____

4. The thing I like most about my friend is_____

_____

_____

_____

_____

5. The thing that bugs me the most about my friend is _____

_____

_____

_____

_____

6. The thing that my friend likes most about me is _____

_____

_____

7. The thing that bugs my friend the most about me is _____

_____

_____

_____

8. When we're together, the things we like to do most are: _____

_____

_____

_____

9. The best time we ever had together was _____

_____

_____

_____

10. The worst fight we ever had was _____

_____

_____

_____

How alike or how different are you and your best friend? The quiz below will help you answer this question. First, you take the quiz and record your answers on page 14. When you have finished, cover up your answers. Have your best friend take the quiz and record his/her answers too. Then, turn to page 14 to score your quizzes.

QUIZ

1. If I had the following choices, I would spend New Year's Eve:
- ☐ **a.** At a big, loud party with lots of friends.
- ☐ **b.** At a small party with my closest friends.
- ☐ **c.** Hiking in the moonlight with a few friends and greeting the New Year from a mountaintop.
- ☐ **d.** Alone with someone I'm dating or with someone I have a crush on.

2. If someone gave me a hundred dollars, I would most likely:
- ☐ **a.** Put it in a savings account.
- ☐ **b.** Buy clothes, makeup, or jewelry.
- ☐ **c.** Spend most, or at least a good part of it, buying presents for others.
- ☐ **d.** Put it towards some major purchase like a musical instrument, a bike, a car, a video machine, a stereo, or some such item.

3. If I went to a party and someone offered me a joint,* I would:
- ☐ **a.** Say, "What's a joint?"
- ☐ **b.** Smoke it.
- ☐ **c.** Say, "No thanks."
- ☐ **d.** Want to leave the party immediately.

4. If I had to choose one of the following as the biggest problem area in my life right now, I would say:
- ☐ **a.** Problems with parents or other relatives.
- ☐ **b.** Problems with school and grades.
- ☐ **c.** Romantic problems.
- ☐ **d.** Other problems.

5. If I were marooned for a month on a desert island, I would most want to have with me (pick one):
- ☐ **a.** A stereo cassette player, tapes, and lots of batteries.
- ☐ **b.** A supply of books to read.
- ☐ **c.** A computer (with enough batteries, of course).
- ☐ **d.** A television set (battery run, of course).

6. Of the following school subjects, which one do you like the most:
- ☐ **a.** English.
- ☐ **b.** Math or science.
- ☐ **c.** Foreign language.
- ☐ **d.** History or social studies.

7. If you had to pick one of the following sets of careers, which would you be most likely to choose:
- ☐ **a.** Doctor/Scientist/Computer Programmer.
- ☐ **b.** Artist/Writer/Actor/Musician.
- ☐ **c.** Dancer/Professional Athlete/Aerobics Instructor.
- ☐ **d.** Teacher/Social Worker/Psychologist.

8. If you could change one thing about your body, you would choose to change your:
- ☐ **a.** Height.
- ☐ **b.** Weight.
- ☐ **c.** Bust or chest measurement.
- ☐ **d.** Face.

9. Which of the following qualities would be most important for someone you were dating to have:
- ☐ **a.** Good looks.
- ☐ **b.** A good sense of humor.
- ☐ **c.** Brains or intelligence.
- ☐ **d.** Sensitivity and kindness.

---

*A "joint" is a marijuana cigarette.

10. Which of the following situations would upset you the most:
- ☐ **a.** Getting a D on your report card.
- ☐ **b.** Breaking up with a boyfriend.
- ☐ **c.** Being grounded for 3 months.
- ☐ **d.** Breaking your arm.

YOUR ANSWERS

Write Your Answers In This Column

1. _____
2. _____
3. _____
4. _____
5. _____
6. _____
7. _____
8. _____
9. _____
10. _____

Cover Your Answers and Have Your Friend Write His/Her Answers In This Column:

1. _____
2. _____
3. _____
4. _____
5. _____
6. _____
7. _____
8. _____
9. _____
10. _____

SCORING YOUR QUIZ

Compare your answers with your friend's answers. If the two of you have given the same answer to a question, give yourself 5 points. Then, add up the total number of points. Example: If you have the same answers for five questions, your total score would be 25 points, if you answered 6 questions the same way, your score would be 30 points, and so on.

If your total number of points is:

35-50 points: It's no wonder that the two of you are friends! You're very much alike, and this is a good basis for a strong friendship. But, friends who are very similar can run into problems, too; because you're so much alike you might tend to compete with each other. You may be so much alike that you have trouble recognizing or accepting the differences you do have. However, you have a lot in common, and this makes for a strong friendship.

15-30 points: In some ways the two of you are very much alike; in other ways, you're very different. The things you have in common strengthen your friendship. The differences you have may also strengthen your friendship and help each of you to grow. It's important, though, that you remember to respect your differences. You've got a good mix here, one that makes for a strong friendship.

0-10 points: Have you ever heard the expression "Opposites attract"? Well, that seems to be the case with the two of you! You're very different kinds of people. And, that's great! Some of the strongest and longest lasting friendships are those between opposites. As long as you don't let your differences come between you, your friendship may last a lifetime.

PROBLEMS WITH BEST FRIENDS

There can be problems, even with the best of friends. There may be times when the two of you fight with each other. But when you think about it, it's not surprising that best friends fight. Any time two people are especially close, there's bound to be some fighting from time to time. In fact, an important part of a friendship is knowing that the two of you can fight and still be friends. When you have a close friend, you can let out angry feelings without having to worry that the friendship will be over. Sometimes having a problem or a fight and making up makes you even closer than ever. Still, while you're in the middle of the fight, it can feel pretty awful. It helps to remember that, as awful as it might feel to fight with your best friend, it's bound to happen at least once in a while.

QUIZ

Below is a list of some of the best friend problems that people have told us about. Put a check next to the problems you've run into. Use the blank spaces at the end of the list to add other problems that you've run into that aren't on this list.

☐ **1.** Your parents don't approve of your best friend and don't like you spending time together, or your best friend's parents don't approve of you.

☐ **2.** Your best friend is a boy. People act like you're weird for having a best friend of the opposite sex. Or people tease you and won't believe that you're "just friends."

☐ **3.** Your best friend acts one way when you're alone and another way when you're in a group of people.

☐ **4.** Your best friend is sometimes thoughtless and makes rude remarks, criticizes you, or does other things that hurt your feelings.

☐ **5.** Your friendship is changing. You just aren't as close as you used to be.

☐ **6.** Your best friend is jealous or possessive and gets hurt if you have other close friends, or you get hurt when your best friend has other close friends.

☐ **7.** Your best friend is too changeable. One day you're best friends; the next day you're not.

☐ **8.** You have two best friends who don't get along with each other. You feel pulled between them.

☐ **9.** Your best friend doesn't keep the secrets you've told him or her.

☐ **10.** You feel really close to your best friend, but hardly anybody else likes him or her. People around you wonder why you're friends with such a weird person.

Other problems:_____

_____

_____

_____

_____

_____

_____

SOLVING THESE PROBLEMS

We wish we had a set of easy solutions for these sorts of problems—you know ... one, two, three, easy-to-follow steps that would fix everything up. We don't. Life, as you may have noticed, is rarely that easy.

We can, however, make one suggestion—find someone to talk the problem over with, perhaps someone older than you might have gone through these same problems and might have some helpful advice. This person might be your mom, your dad, an older brother or sister, a teacher, or someone else to whom you feel close.

If you simply go up to the person you've decided to talk to about these problems and say, "Hey, I've got this problem and I want your advice," you might get some helpful advice. But, then again, you might not, as this girl explains:

> *I try to talk to my mom about problems with my best friend. All my mom ever says is, "Well, if she's going to act like that find someone else to be friends with."*

This kind of advice isn't very helpful. One way to avoid getting this kind of not-very-helpful advice is to actually do an interview with whomever you choose to ask for advice. The interview questions below will get the person you're interviewing to remember how it was when they were your age and will get them to think seriously about your problems. This will increase your chances of having a really good talk and of getting some helpful advice. You don't have to ask these exact questions in this exact way, but these questions should get you off to a good start.

INTERVIEW

1. When you were my age did you have a best friend? If so, tell me about this person? Who was s/he? How did the two of you get to be friends? What did you like about this person?

_____

_____

_____

2. Do you still know this person? If so, how often do you see him or her? How do you stay in touch with each other? If not, how and why did the two of you end your friendship or lose touch with each other?

_____

_____

_____

3. I'd like to read you a list of problems people sometimes have with their best friends. (Turn to the list of problems on page 15, and read it aloud.) Did you and your best friend ever run into any of these problems or any other problems? If so, how did you feel about it at the time? How do you feel about it now that you're older? How did things turn out? If you had this same problem today, would you handle it any differently?

_____

_____

_____

4. Right now, I'm having a problem with my best friend. (Explain one or more of the problems you're having and how you feel about the problem.) Did you ever have this problem or a similar one? If so, tell me about it. How did you handle the problem? What would you do if you were me? What advice do you have for me?

_____

_____

_____

2: POPULARITY, IN-CROWDS, AND MAKING FRIENDS

In addition to telling us about their best friends, the preteens and teens we interviewed also talked to us about their other friendships. In these interviews, we heard a lot of different ideas and opinions on topics like popularity, the group scene, in-crowds, and making friends. In this section we will be telling you what some of the people we interviewed had to say on these topics. We'll also be asking you to think and write about your feelings, thoughts, and ideas.

Popularity

Being popular means being well-liked and accepted by the people around you. For some people, being popular is very important. For others, it's not such a big deal.

Exercise

Here are short descriptions of six different girls' feelings toward popularity. We'd like you to read through each of these descriptions and decide which girl comes closest to your own thoughts and feelings about popularity.

Lisa

Lisa has a lot of friends and is one of the most popular girls in her class. She's well liked because she's such a nice person. She goes out of her way to be friendly to everyone, even to people who aren't very popular. People like and respect her for this. She enjoys her popularity. It means that she always has friends to do things with. It makes her feel happy and important when people say hi to her in the halls. She enjoys being the center of so much attention.

Evonne

Although she's liked by some people, Evonne isn't one of the real popular girls at her school. This doesn't, however, bother Evonne. Her basic attitude is "I don't like everybody, so why should everybody like me?" She has a few close friends who are important to her, but she doesn't really care about being popular.

Holly

Looking at it from the outside, it would seem that Holly is very popular. She's part of the so-called "in-crowd" at her school. She's always with a group and she's always invited to all the parties. But Holly herself often feels lonely or out of it, like she doesn't really belong. Even though it seems like she's well liked and accepted, Holly doesn't really feel like she's popular.

Katie

Katie, too, is part of the most popular group at her school. But she doesn't always feel real great about her popularity. Sometimes she's afraid to do or say certain things because she's afraid she'll lose "popularity points." She's afraid that other people won't like her anymore unless she acts a certain way.

Wendy

Wendy describes herself as being "one of the most popular girls in my not-very-popular group." She's not part of the in-crowd, but among her set of friends, she's well liked. She's not too impressed by the popular crowd, either. She thinks a lot of them are stuck up and that they're often mean to other, unpopular kids. "If that's what it takes to be popular, I'd rather just skip it" is Wendy's attitude.

Tracy

Tracy feels like a tag-a-long. She's sort of on the edges of the popular group, but she's not really "in." She sometimes feels that the other girls would just as soon not have her around. She'd give anything to be more accepted and more popular. She often feels depressed or hurt because she's not popular.

Ellen

Ellen doesn't really have any friends at all. She's very shy, and it's hard for her to get to know people. She wishes she were popular and well liked by everyone. But she'd settle for having just one or two friends.

1. Which of these girls is most like you? How are you like her?_____

_____

_____

_____

_____

2. Which of these girls is least like you? How is she different?_____

_____

_____

_____

_____

3. Which of these girls would you most want to be like? Why would you want to be like her?_____

_____

_____

_____

_____

_____

_____

If, like Ellen, you wish you had more friends, you might like to read the section "Making Friends." If, like Holly, Katie, and Wendy, your school has certain groups or in-crowds, you might want to read the next section, "The Group Scene."

THE GROUP SCENE

When we interviewed young people and asked them to talk to us about popularity, about the social scene at their school, and about their relationships with the other kids they knew, we heard a lot about "in-crowds" and what one teenager called "the group scene."

Belonging or not belonging to a certain group or in-crowd seems to be a very important part of the lives of many of the preteens and teens we interviewed. Of course, belonging to groups is an important part of everyone's life, young and old alike. But, fitting in, being accepted by, and belonging to a certain group can be especially important during our growing-up years. Some of the young people we interviewed said that they were part of a group, crowd, or clique of friends who ran around together, who did things with each other, or who simply "hung out" together. Some said that they were on the edges or "fringes" of such a group or crowd. Others said that they belonged to a number of different groups or crowds at their school. Still others said that they were "out of it" or didn't belong to any of these sorts of groups or in-crowds. But, regardless of whether they were "in" or "out" of these groups, most kids said that there were one or more cliques or "in-crowds" at their schools.

Some of the people we interviewed had good things to say about these sorts of groups or crowds. Others weren't so happy with the group scene. In this section, we'll be sharing with you some of the positive and negative things the people we interviewed had to say about the group scene and asking you to write about your own opinions and feelings in regard to the group scene. But, before we start talking about the good and bad aspects of groups, we'd like you to think about the group scene at your school.

The group scene—different people relate to it in different ways.

Some kids said that they were the leaders or at least part of a certain in-crowd or group at their school.

Some said that they were "on the edge" or "fringes" of such a crowd.

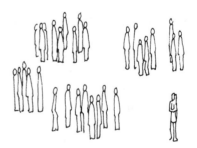

Others said that they belonged to a number of different groups or cliques

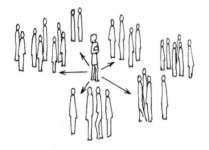

Still others said that they were "out of it" and didn't belong to any of the groups or in-crowds at their school.

THE GROUP SCENE AT YOUR SCHOOL

The group scene works differently at different schools. Some kids said that there was a really strong group scene at their school. Others said that the group scene wasn't so strong. Below are some quotes from kids whom we asked to describe the group scene at their schools. Deanna, a fifth grader, explained her group in this way:

There's this group of girls who I run around with. There's Amy and me. Amy's my best friend. There's Gigi and Felicia who are best friends. There's Vanessa and Irene and Elena and they're all three best friends. . . . So, my group is made up of a group of best friends who are all in the same grade and we eat lunch together and go over to each other's houses and stuff like that.

Mandy, a seventh grader, had this to say:

In my grade there's different groups of kids. There's the most popular group and they all go around together. They kind of run things. I'm friends with some of those kids, but mostly I run around with a group that's second most popular.

Some kids said that the groups at their schools revolved around being on a sports team, being involved in student government, being in band or choir or being on a school newspaper or yearbook staff. Fifteen-year-old Tara described it this way:

I'm in band and choir, and the kids in the music department all hang out together. We have music in common and we spend a lot of time in rehearsals and stuff, so we're together a lot. We all go to the same parties . . . It's really neat. It's like a big family. You're automatically part of the group because you're in the music department.

A number of kids said that the group scene at their schools had a lot to do with what kind of classes or courses a person took or what kind of school activities a person was involved in. Elaine, a tenth grader, explained it this way:

Kids in my school have different majors—college prep, accelerated, business, vocational. The different majors each have certain groups. Like there's certain crowds among the business kids, certain crowds among the college prep and shop [vocational] kids. Some kids mix with kids in different majors, but mostly it's divided up according to what courses you're taking. Then within each major it's divided up like the most popular of the college prep kids who hang out together and then there's the next most popular group and so on.

Another teenager described the group scene at her school in this way:

It's not like there's any one in-crowd. There's lots of different crowds, like there's the surfers, the rah-rah-kids—who are like cheerleaders and into student council and school spirit—the preppies, the mods, heavy metal crowd, stoners, band kids, drama kids—the ones who take drama and get in all the plays—the jocks . . . It's a regular zoo!

Other kids said that the group scene at their school wasn't so strong. One junior high student whom we asked to tell us about the social scene at her school said this:

> *It's not such a big deal really. There are certain kids who are just natu-*
> *rally friends with each other, but people aren't really divided up into these*
> *definite little groups. But, I'm only in junior high and maybe it gets*
> *different later on. . . . My sister's a junior and at the high school it is*
> *more divided up. People are more separated into groups, so maybe it*
> *will happen that way for me when I get older.*

Some kids said that they were part of a group that was made up of kids who weren't in groups or who were in rebellion against the group scene, like this school senior who said:

> *I really started noticing it in junior high. There were the most popular*
> *kids who all sat in a certain place at lunch time. I wasn't really part of*
> *that group. I was in with a group—mostly girls—who didn't like the*
> *group thing. We were down on the whole business of groups. We thought*
> *that we were individuals and we looked down on the groups, like it was*
> *really dumb. But, really, we were a group—a group of kids who were*
> *against groups.*

Although most of the kids we interviewed said that there was some sort of group scene at their school, there were some kids, like fourteen-year-old Matt, who said that there really wasn't a group scene at their school:

> *I go to an alternative school and groups kind of go against the philoso-*
> *phy. Besides, it's so small that there really couldn't be groups. Everyone's*
> *just friends with everyone else.*

FREEWRITING EXERCISE

Is there a group scene at your school? How does the group scene work? Are there one or more in-crowds? Are you "in" or "out" of the group? How do you feel about the group and about belonging (or not belonging) to a group? Use the blank space below to freewrite about the group scene at your school, about the group or groups you belong to, about the other kids in the group, or about how you feel about the group scene.

_____

_____

_____

_____

_____

_____

_____

_____

_____

_____

THE GOOD THINGS ABOUT BELONGING TO A GROUP

The kids who said that they belonged to a certain crowd or clique often had good things to say about belonging to groups, which is hardly surprising. After all, why would there even be such a thing as the group scene if groups didn't have something going for them?

One thing that people said over and over was that being part of a group helped them feel less alone. If you're part of a group you don't have to sit alone at lunch time or home all by yourself on Saturday night. You've got a gang of friends to do things with, and this can be very important. Doing certain things, like going to the movies or football game, wouldn't be much fun if we had to do them by ourselves. But, if we do these sorts of things with a group of friends, we can have a lot of fun.

Having a group of friends to share the good times with makes those good times all the more fun. Having a group of friends to share things with can also make the hard times a little easier, as this girl explains:

> _My parents got divorced last year. It was really terrible. I love them both so much, but I couldn't really talk to them about everything I was going through . . . I guess they were going through too much to really be there for me. I had my friends. Thank god . . . I could talk to them and cry and they listened to me. Some of the kids in my crowd had been divorced too, so they knew what I was going through. I don't think I could have gotten through it without my friends._

Another positive thing about being part of a group is that the group can give us the courage to try things we might not have the courage to try on our own. One boy told us that he was too shy to get out on the dance floor, but his friends helped him "get up his nérve" and get out there and try dancing. A fourteen-year-old girl said:

> _I wasn't going to go out for the school play, but all my friends were trying out. They said, "Hey come on, we're all gonna try out." At first I wasn't gonna—I didn't want to get up there and look like a fool. They all said,_

*"Come on, we're all gonna make fools of ourselves, you do it too." So, I
went and I got a part!*

Many kids said that being part of a group made it easier to be "just friends"
with someone of the opposite sex, as this girl explains:

*Usually you're only friends with a boy if you're dating him or he's your
boyfriend. But, I'm part of a group—there's maybe ten girls and eight
guys—and none of us date each other. We're just friends. Some of us
have boyfriends or girlfriends, but in the group it's "just friends", which
is nice because you can be friends with a boy without it being all
romantic.*

Being part of a group can also help us feel more sure of ourselves and more
self-confident. One fifty-year-old man told us that he'd been part of a group of
seven or eight boys who were friends all through grade school, junior high and
high school:

*We were inseparable, together night and day. And, I'll tell you some-
thing, to this day, I still have a sense of security about myself that comes
from the friendship and support I got from that group of guys while I
was growing up. I'm not a wealthy man. I'm not the chief executive offi-
cer of a big corporation. Inside, though, I feel wealthy. I feel very se-
cure about myself. I think my friendships with those boys has a lot to do
with this.*

Another nice thing about groups is that they give us a sense of belonging or
"fitting in," which can be really important during our growing years. For one
thing, many of us change schools during these years, going from grade school to
junior high or from junior high to senior high. Changing from the old school to
the new one can be exciting, but also scary. Being part of a group or gang of
friends can make this change a lot easier, as this girl explains:

*I was really nervous about starting junior high because my grade school
was really small and the junior high school had so many more kids. I
didn't know if I'd fit in. I was afraid that I'd be really out of it. At first,
I didn't know anybody. Then, I got in with this certain group. Being part
of the group helped me fit in. I had friends so I felt more like I belonged.*

Belonging to a group gives us a sense of identity. As we get older and less
attached to our families, friends become more important. We are, as the saying
goes, "leaving the nest." We're "trying our wings." We're finding out how people
outside our family will respond to us—Will they like us? Are we acceptable? Are
we okay? We're asking that all-important question, "Who am I?" Being part of a
group can help us answer these questions, as this girl explains:

Sure your mom and dad and your brothers and sisters like you, but they're your family. They have to like you. But, will other people like you? . . . When you're part of a group, you know at least these people think you're okay and accept you!

Or, as another put it:

You're trying to figure out, like, "Who am I?", "What kind of person am I?" and you don't really know yet 'cause you're still growing up and trying to figure it out . . . The other kids in your clique are like you, so you can say, Well, who am I?—one of the things I am is this kind of person who goes around with these kinds of people. So, it's kind of an answer.

As we say, belonging to a group has a lot of advantages and there are certainly many good things to be said about the group scene. But, there are also other, not-so-great things about groups and in the next few pages we'll be talking about some of the negative aspects of groups.

THE NOT-SO-GREAT THINGS ABOUT THE GROUP SCENE

Although many of the people we interviewed had good things to say about groups, there were also many people who had complaints about the group scene. One of the biggest complaints that we heard was that groups or cliques often make kids who *aren't* in feel bad. One mother talked to us about her preteen daughter:

My daughter would just die to be in with this gang of snotty little girls at her school. When they snub her or she's not included in one of their parties, it just destroys her. I ache for her. I'd like to wring their necks. I really would. It makes my daughter feel horrible about herself. It's just so cruel.

We heard countless stories from young people, telling us how hurt and rejected they felt and how they suffered because they weren't accepted by a certain group. If you've ever felt this way, it might be helpful for you to think about what one grown-up we interviewed had to say:

You know, being "in" with the in-crowd can be such a big deal when you're a kid, but it really doesn't have anything to do with what your life will be like when you're older. The kids who were in the in-crowd in my high school days—most of them never amounted to much, whereas this kid who was a science nerd now runs a billion dollar computer business. And, one of the girls in my class is now a famous model. She wasn't even pretty in high school. In fact, she was a real wallflower. So

kids shouldn't pay too much attention to what goes on in junior and se-
nior high school. Things change. People change. Situations change.

Although it's true that being in with a certain clique can make you feel less
lonely, being in doesn't always make your life so wonderful, as this thirteen-year-
old explains:

I have a bunch of friends—popular kids—and I like them and all. But,
I still feel left out. I feel like I don't quite fit in. I go along with them and
laugh and act like I'm having a good time, but inside I feel empty and
out of it.

Even people who weren't hurt by not being included in a certain clique had
complaints about the group scene. One woman told us that she thought the group
scene divided people up and kept people from getting to know one another. She
said:

By junior high, you got divided up into kids who were taking college
prep, kids who were taking business and secretarial majors, kids who were
in majors like auto mechanics, graphic arts, and so on. There were a
few kids who managed to cross in the lines and be part of a crowd of kids
who had a different major. But, mostly, people stuck to their own kind,
which was too bad really because you didn't ever get to know people who
were different from you.

A teenage girl who wrote to us also thought that the group scene divided
people up and made it harder for people to be friends with each other. She
described a sort of "war between the groups" at her school:

At my school there's this group and that group. The girls in one group
gossip about the girls in the other group and everything. . . . It's like if
you're a member of one group, then you're automatically enemies with
the girls in the other group. I'd like to be friends with different people, but
if you do that, you're not part of any group.

A lot of the young people we talked to said that the group scene was a drag
because it was hard to belong to more than one group at once. Some kids said
that you were excluded by other groups once you started hanging around with
one certain group. Other kids said that being part of more than one crowd
meant you weren't really in the center of any group, as this fourteen-year-old
explains:

I'm friends with kids in several different crowds, but it's like I'm not
really in the center of any of them because I divide myself up. So, if one
group has a party, I'm not automatically invited like I would be if that

was the only group I was in. . . . I have to make an effort to be included in their plans because I'm not always around the same group all the time.

The kids we interviewed also complained that people tend to label you or stick you into a certain category because you were part of a particular crowd, as this thirteen-year-old explains:

I'm a cheerleader and I'm in with a crowd of kids who are on the squad and on the sports team or active in student government and clubs, you know, kids who have a lot of school spirit. But, a lot of times, other people act like I'm just some rah-rah dumb blonde. Like in class discussions, they don't take my opinions seriously because they think that because I'm a cheerleader, I must be totally brainless.

A fifteen-year-old boy also said that he felt he was labeled:

My friends and I have a bad reputation, and it's true we get into trouble sometimes. It makes me mad, though, because every time something goes wrong, my friends and I automatically get blamed for it 'cause everyone thinks the kids in my crowd are such troublemakers.

Another girl, an eleven-year-old, also felt she'd been stuck in a category because of the group scene:

The girls in my clique—we all get good grades. We have a reputation for being brains, and then that's all people ever see about us. We like to have fun and get crazy sometimes. But because we get good grades, everyone thinks, "Oh, they're serious. They're always studying. They're no fun."

Another big problem with the group scene has to do with something called peer pressure. Peer pressure means being pressured or talked into doing (or not doing) something by your friends. There's sometimes a lot of pressure on the members of the groups to go along with or conform to the group's ideas and wishes which may, at times, be different from your own, individual ideas and wishes. Peer pressure was a problem for many of the young people we interviewed. In fact, there were so many kids who talked to us about peer pressure that we decided to do a separate section on peer pressure. But, before you turn to that section, we'd like you to try the freewriting exercise below.

FREEWRITING EXERCISE

Now that you've heard what other people think about the advantages and disadvantages of the group scene, we'd like you to write about your own ideas. What do you think about the group scene? What are the good things and the not-so-great things about groups? Of course, since this is a freewriting exercise, you don't have to answer these particular questions, just keep the topic of the group scene and what you read in mind. Start writing and don't stop until you've filled up all the empty space.

_____

_____

_____

_____

_____

_____

_____

_____

_____

_____

_____

Making Friends

Some people seem to have a knack or a gift for making friends. For others, it's more difficult. Take, for example, these boys and girls who wrote to us about their problems in making friends:

I'm too shy. I don't know what to say to people. I don't have any friends. What should I do?

—ten-year-old girl

I wish I was popular, but how does a person like me get friends?

—eleven-year-old girl

I haven't got many friends. How do you make a friend?

—thirteen-year-old boy

I'm nice and I think I could be a good friend for someone to have. People don't accept me. I don't know how to get them to like me.

—twelve-year-old boy

Suppose these boys and girls had written to you? What advice could you give them on how to make friends? See if you can think up at least five tips.

1. _____

2. _____

3. _____

4. _____

5. _____

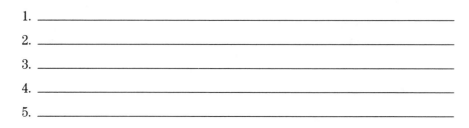

EXERCISE

Now that you've thought about what advice you'd give someone who wanted to know how to make friends, take a look below and you'll see what advice the people we interviewed had. If your advice agrees with theirs, put a check mark in the box. Or, if you're having trouble making friends and this advice seems like something that would work for you, put a check mark in the box.

☐ **1.** *Join, Join, Join!* Most people thought that joining a club or activity at school, a youth group at church or temple, a volunteer organization in the community, or some other young people's group was the best way to meet people and make friends.

If you have a special interest—whether it's stamp collecting, chess, computers, a foreign language, or whatever—find out if there's a club that centers around the activity and join. If you have a specific career in mind for yourself, check to see if there's a Future Teachers, Future Physicians, 4-H Club, or some other career-oriented club at your school—and join up.

If you have a special talent, say in music, drama, or athletics, you might try out for the band, choir, orchestra, cheerleading squad, a school play, or a sports team. Even if you don't make the team, land a part in the play, or get a place in the band, you still may be able to play a role in these sorts of activities. You might, for instance, offer to be a stagehand, to paint scenery, or to make costumes for the school play. You might assist the band manager. You might become the bat girl for the softball team or the timer or scorer for the hockey team.

Does your school have a newspaper, a yearbook, or a literary magazine? Here again, you don't have to be the world's greatest writer to join. These staffs always need typists, proofreaders, layout people, advertising salespeople, and business managers.

What about community service groups? Hospitals, old folks' homes, homes for disabled children, and other such places often have groups of young volunteers. Not only will you be helping yourself by meeting other volunteers your own age, you'll also be helping others, too. Or, how about your local YWCA or other community organization? If they don't have a young people's volunteer service group, they'll be able to tell you who does.

We could go on and on, but you get the idea—find a group and join!

□ **2.** *Throw a party!* It might be a slumber party, a boy–girl party, a birthday party; a Halloween, Valentine's Day, or Christmas party. (Of course, your parents will have to go along with your plans.) Once word gets around that you're having a party, you'll be surprised how many people get friendly. After all, everyone loves a party. One woman whose father was in the Army and who went to five different schools in junior and senior high told us:

> *As soon as we'd move to a new town and I at least knew some people's names, I'd have a slumber party. People would sometimes act shocked— "You're inviting me to a party—I don't even hardly know you." Usually, though, they'd turn up. My mom would be great with all kinds of dumb party games, scavenger hunts, and stuff to break the ice. We'd eat pizza and play records and stay up all night and suddenly I'd have a bunch of friends.*

□ **3.** *Figure out who you want to be friends with—and why.* Several of the adults we talked to thought this was an important step in making friends. They pointed out that some kids pick the people they want to be friends with on the basis of things like looks or popularity. But, if you pick friends on this sort of basis, you may run into trouble. What's more important is whether the person is nice, whether the two of you could be comfortable with each other, could trust each other, could have fun with each other, and could be honest with each other. These inner qualities in a friend are much more important than outer qualities like whether the person's pretty or popular.

Several people also suggested that a person who's having trouble making friends might want to take a careful look at the people around them. Is there someone around you who's often alone or who doesn't seem to have a lot of friends? Maybe that person is shy. Perhaps that person would be more open to making friends than someone who already has a lot of friends.

□ **4.** *Don't be shy.* A lot of people come up with advice like "Smile," "Be friendly," "Show an interest in others," "Start conversations," "Introduce yourself"—in short, don't be shy.

Of course, this is a lot easier said than done, especially if you're a person who's kind of shy anyhow. It helps to remember that everyone has a shy side. Even kids who are outgoing have times when they feel shy. If you feel shy, you're definitely not alone!

But, unless you make an effort to get over your shyness, you won't be able to meet people and make friends. If you're very shy, you might want to start out simply saying, "Hi," and smiling at people in the halls, on the school bus, or wherever. Let people know you're alive!

Starting a conversation with someone we don't know very well is a difficult thing to do. But, remember that it doesn't have to be the world's longest or most brilliant conversation. You can start out with simple things like, "How did you do on the math test?"; "What are you writing for your English paper?"; "Who won the football game last week?"; "Who do you have for social studies?"; or simply, "Hi, my name's _____, what's yours?"

One woman told us:

> *I was so shy when I was a teenager. I was literally painfully shy. I would go to school, never make so much as a peep in class unless the teacher called on me. I would go through the whole day and go home after school, never having said a word to anyone else. I was miserably lonely. Finally, I just made up my mind—and my mother encouraged me, prodded me. I made up my mind that I was going to say "hi" to five people every day, no matter what. Then I got up my nerve to say a sentence or two, you know, to the person whose locker was next to mine or someone sitting next to me. It took a long time, but finally I did get to know people and made some friends.*

It isn't easy to overcome shyness, but if you want to make friends, you have to make the effort.

☐ **5.** *Don't be afraid to take the first step.* People said this in a lot of different ways: "Ask someone to eat lunch with you;" "Invite someone to come over to your home after school;" "See if someone wants to do homework or study for a test with you;" "Ask someone to go to the movies."

In some ways, this is a lot like the last piece of advice about not being shy. It can be very scary to take the first step because the person you're talking to might say no. The person might not want to come over to your house or to eat lunch with you or do whatever it is that you're suggesting. Being turned down can really hurt your feelings. But if you want to have friends, you have to be willing to risk being hurt and to take the first step.

Let's say that you do finally get up the nerve to ask someone to do something with you, and the person says no. Don't go running off with your tail between your legs and your feelings hurt. Maybe there's a real reason why the person can't. If he or she turns you down because of a dentist appointment, a music lesson, an appointment in the counselor's office, or some such thing, you might say, "Well, how about tomorrow or some other time?" If the person still doesn't respond to your invitation, it may be that he or she really doesn't want to get to know you—or it may be something else altogether, having nothing to do with you. For example, if you've asked someone to come over to your house after school, it could be that the person's parents make him or her come straight home from school and he or she is embarrassed to tell you that. So try suggesting something else.

One suggestion that people had was that you ask the person in private, not in front of a whole group of kids. Sometimes a person may want to do something with you but be afraid to say so in front of friends. If you ask the person in private, you'll have a better chance of getting a yes answer.

Finally, if you keep asking and keep getting turned down, try another person. After all, even though it hurts to be turned down, it's really not the end of the world, is it? Hang in there. Sooner or later you'll find someone who wants to be your friend.

3: PEER PRESSURE

One topic that came up over and over again when we talked to young people about popularity, friendships, and belonging to a certain group or crowd was peer pressure. Peer pressure means being pressured, influenced, convinced, or talked into doing (or not doing) something by someone else. (The word "peer" means your equals, your friends, other kids you know, or just kids in general who are about the same age as you.)

Another way of putting it is to say that peer pressure means going against your true feelings or not acting according to what you think is the right thing to do because of what your friends might think or do or say. We could spend about ten pages trying to give you a perfectly exact definition of peer pressure, but probably the best way to explain it is to give you a few examples:

• Sally's friends all think that heavy metal rock is totally awesome. Sally thinks it sounds like a lot of noise. She prefers classical music. But Sally pretends to like heavy metal rock because her friends do. She doesn't say what she really thinks about heavy metal rock or talk about how she prefers classical music because she's afraid her friends will think she's "out of it" or "un-cool." Peer pressure keeps Sally from expressing her real feelings.

Peer pressure takes many forms.   One of the commonest, unfortunately, goes like: "Oh, don't be such a baby—try it!"

• Angela and Norman have been next-door neighbors since they were just little kids. Norman is not exactly what you'd call "cool." He looks and acts like something out of *Revenge of the Nerds*. But, Norman is really a neat (if a bit unusual) sort of guy, once you get to know him. Angela's friends at school all think Norman is completely weird. They can't believe that Angela is friends with him. As a result, Angela is sometimes embarrassed about Norman and acts like she hardly knows him, even though they've been friends for a long time. Peer pressure makes Angela embarrassed and makes her downplay or ignore her friendship with Norman.

• Jeanette runs around with a crowd of kids who smoke cigarettes, drink alcohol, and sometimes smoke pot. Jeanette doesn't really think smoking, drinking, or taking drugs are good ideas. Her parents would flip out if they knew she'd done these things. But, when she's at parties or is hanging out with her friends, she often does these things, even though she doesn't really want to. She's afraid her friends will think she's not cool or that they won't want her to be part of their crowd if she doesn't do these things. Peer pressure influences Jeanette to do things that she really doesn't want to do.

Everybody—adults and kids alike—have times in their lives when they let peer pressure affect their behavior. Of course, some people are more affected by peer pressure than others, and even the same person may react differently to peer pressure at different times, depending on the circumstances. The quiz below will help you think about how much peer pressure affects your life.

QUIZ

Below are ten situations in which peer pressure plays a role. Some of these situations may sound like something that happened to you when you were younger. Some may sound like something that's happened more recently, and some may sound like a situation you might run into when you're a bit older. Even if you have never been in the situation described, or if it doesn't sound like anything that would ever happen to you, we'd like you to use your imagination and to pretend for a few minutes that you are actually in it.

After each of the situations, there are three possible reactions or ways to handle the case described. Read through each situation and pick the choice that is closest to what you think you might do if you found yourself in that situation. None of the choices may be exactly what you'd do, just pick the one that comes closest to describing how you might react or behave.

Take your time. Think carefully before you make your choice, and remember—be honest! Don't pick the answer that you think you *should* pick or that you think is the "right" answer. Pick the answer that comes closest to describing how you'd really act if you were in that situation.

1. Your mom gives you a new purse for your birthday. You think the purse is really neat and you like it a lot. But, when you take it to school, one of your friends says, "Where in the world did you get that thing?" Another girl you know says, "Nobody carries purses like that anymore!" Other kids also say things that let you know that they think your purse is kind of weird. If this happened to you, how would you react?

☐ **a.** Decide that you really don't like the purse after all. Take it home, stick it in the back of your closet, and never use it again.

☐ **b.** Even though you still like the purse, you don't take it to school anymore, or you only take it once in awhile. You might use it when you're going somewhere with your parents or other adults. But, as a rule, you don't use it when you're going to be around other kids who might think it's weird.

☐ **c.** Figure that, despite what the other kids have said, you like the purse and that's what really counts. You continue using the purse and taking it to school every day, either ignoring or laughing off the comments the other kids make.

2. Your dad was on the debating team at school when he was your age. He makes it sound like a lot of fun. He encourages you to get involved in debating. There's a debate club at your school and you're thinking about joining. When you mention this idea to your friends, they say things like. "Are you kidding? Only a total nerd would join that club!" or "If you join the debate club everybody will think you're weird. Nobody's going to want to be friends with you if you start hanging around with those nerds." If you were in this situation, how would you react?

☐ **a.** Decide that joining the debate club isn't really such a great idea after all and forget about your plans for joining.

☐ **b.** Go ahead and join the debate club, but you don't talk much about the club and its activities around your friends. In other words, you don't advertise the fact that you've joined. You don't exactly keep it a secret, but you sort of downplay the fact that you're a member of the club. You usually avoid bringing the topic of the debate club up around your friends.

☐ **c.** Decide that you're still interested in joining, no matter what other people think. You join up and don't bother to downplay the fact or to avoid mentioning it around friends. You talk to your friends about the club and its activities, just as you would talk about anything else that was happening in your life.

3. There's a very unattractive, overweight girl in your class whom we'll call Phyllis. It's not just her looks that make Phyllis unattractive; her personality isn't too great either. In fact, she can be kind of obnoxious. Sometimes, she shows off how smart she is or brags about how rich her family is. She's also kind of whiney and complains to teachers about how the other kids treat her. One day, you're talking with a bunch of your friends and a couple of kids start making jokes about Phyllis. Everyone starts laughing. Although you don't really like Phyllis, you feel kind of sorry for her. You don't think she's as awful as kids make her out to be. You think she wouldn't be half bad if kids would just give her a chance. But, if you say this, the other kids might think you're weird for sticking up for her. You also think that the reason Phyllis acts the way she does is because other people are so mean to her, but you're afraid the other kids will think you're some kind of goody-goody or preacher if you tell them to lay off. So, what do you do?

☐ **a.** You laugh, too, or at least give a little smile. Maybe you don't laugh as long or as hard as the other kids, but you at least give enough of a smile to make the other kids think you're going along with them and you're "in" on the joke too.

☐ **b.** You don't laugh or act like you're "in" on the joke, but you don't ac-tually come out and say anything either.

☐ **c.** You don't laugh. In fact, you let the other kids know that you don't think it's really OK to make jokes and mean comments about Phyllis.

4. You have a totally mad crush on a certain boy. He's very popular and he's a real hunk. You think maybe he's interested in you too, but you're not really sure. You've just finished taking a big math test, which he'll be taking the next period. As you're leaving the math classroom, he comes up and asks you to tell him about the questions and answers on the test. You could easily give him the answers; however, you really don't feel good about the idea of cheating. This guy is really pressuring you. "Come on," he says, "couldn't you just help me out a little bit? If I don't do well on this test, I may flunk math." You like this guy a lot and don't want to say "no" to him; on the other hand, you don't want to cheat. So, what do you do?

☐ **a.** Give him the answers. Maybe you figure: "What the heck, it's only this one time," or "He's really in trouble and I don't want him to flunk," or "I really like him and I don't want to ruin my chances," or some combination of these things. In any case, you do give him the answers to the test.

☐ **b.** Act like you don't hear him, don't understand what he's asking, or are in too much of a rush to answer him. Or, you make up an excuse or a lie, saying something along the lines of "Oh, it wasn't a hard test," or "Wow, I think I flunked; I don't know the right answers," or "Gee, I can't even remember exactly what the questions were." At any rate, you avoid giving him the answers, without actually saying no.

☐ **c.** You say something like, "Gee, I wouldn't feel O.K. about that," or "No way, that's cheating," or "Gosh, I couldn't do that." In any case, you make it clear that you're not going to cheat.

5. When you were younger, you were best friends with a girl we'll call Robyn. But, nowadays, the two of you hardly ever see each other. You just sort of drifted apart as you grew older and each of you went your separate ways. For one thing, Robyn runs around with an entirely different crowd of kids than you do. Her friends get in a lot of trouble at school. They smoke, take drugs, drink, and are pretty wild. Robyn has a really bad reputation. The kids in your crowd really look down on Robyn's crowd. They especially look down on Robyn and think she's one of the "worst" of the kids in her crowd. You know that the kids in your crowd would be surprised if they knew you'd been friends with Robyn. They might think that you're weird for having been friends with her or that you used to be like her. You're a little embarrassed about your former friendship. How might you handle things if you were in this situation:

☐ **a.** You do your best not to let anyone know that you and Robyn were ever friends. You never mention your old friendship to any of the kids in your crowd. You do your best to avoid Robyn. Sometimes you even pretend not to see her, so you won't have to say "hi."

☐ **b.** You don't avoid Robyn on purpose, but you never say "hi" unless she says something first. You don't run the other way when you see her coming, but when you do run into her, you keep it short and sweet.

☐ **c.** You make a point of being friendly to Robyn whenever you see her. You go out of your way to say "hi" and have a conversation now and then. If you're with one of your friends when you run into Robyn, you make sure that you introduce them to each other.

6. Your English teacher has called on several kids to give their ideas and opinions on a story the class has been reading. So far, everyone who's spoken has expressed pretty much the same opinions. One boy, whom we'll call Robert, has been madly waving his hand, trying to get the teacher to call on him. Robert is, to say the least, not very popular. In fact, most of the kids, including you, can't stand him! For one thing, he's a real know-it-all. He always acts like he's totally brilliant and everyone else is totally stupid. The teacher calls on Robert and he gives his opinion, which (as usual) is completely opposite from everyone else's. And (also as usual), the way he gives his opinion makes it sound as if the other kids' opinions are wrong and just plain dumb. The other kids get angry and start arguing against Robert's ideas. Things get pretty heated. The class is really ganging up on Robert. Some kids make it sound as if anyone with opinions like Robert is just automatically a jerk. The teacher then calls on you and asks your opinion. The problem is that you happen to agree with Robert's opinion! But, you're worried that people will think you're a jerk if you agree with Robert or that you're "on his side." You're afraid they'll be as mad at you as they are at him. Still, the truth of the matter is that you do have strong opinions that you'd like to express, even though they do happen to be very similar to Robert's. If you were in this situation, which of these three choices comes closest to what you might do?

☐ **a.** No way are you going to say what you really think! You give an opinion that's pretty much the same as everyone else's. You don't let on that you really agree with the unpopular Robert and his unpopular ideas.

☐ **b.** You don't actually go so far as to lie and pretend that your opinion is the same as the other kids'. But, you don't let on that your opinion is really the same as the one Robert's been giving either. Perhaps you avoid giving any opinion at all, but, no way do you risk losing "popularity points" by admitting that your ideas are anywhere near Robert's.

☐ **c.** You give your real opinion, even though it means "being on Robert's side" and even though the other kids may get mad at you. You might try to make it clear that, unlike Robert, you don't think other kids' opinions are "wrong" or "dumb." But, you do make it clear to everyone just what your opinion is.

7. You go over to a friend's house after school with a bunch of kids. Your friend's mother smokes and there's a pack of her cigarettes lying around. Someone lights up and begins passing the cigarette around. Everyone is taking turns smoking. Some kids light up cigarettes of their own. You've never smoked before. You know your parents would kill you if they found out you'd been smoking. Besides, you've already decided that smoking isn't something you ever want to do. But everyone else is trying it. When it comes to your turn, everyone says, "Go on, don't be a chicken." If you were faced with this decision, what would you do?

☐ **a.** Go ahead and smoke the cigarette, even though it's not something you really feel good about doing.

☐ **b.** Make up an excuse or a lie to avoid smoking the cigarette like, "I have a sore throat," or "The last time I smoked, it made me sick. I think I must be allergic."

☐ **c.** Just say, "No thanks," or "I'll pass," or "I don't want to."

8. There are two very popular girls in your class who are sort of the leaders of the "in-crowd" at your school. Lately, these girls have been acting really friendly toward you and inviting you to eat lunch with them, come over to their houses after school, and so forth. These two girls really have it in for a third girl in your class whom we'll call Alicia. They're always putting Alicia down, doing mean things to her, snubbing her, and picking fights. You've never been best friends with Alicia, but you have been friendly with her and you do like her. The problem is that these two girls seem to expect you to join in when they start gossiping and putting Alicia down and to be on their side when fights and other incidents come up. You feel that if you don't do these things, these girls won't want to be your friend, or at least they won't want you to be one of their really close friends. If you were to go so far as to stick up for Alicia, you're afraid they won't like you at all. So, what do you do?

☐ **a.** You don't exactly join in when these girls are ganging up on Alicia, but you certainly don't stick up for her. And to tell the truth, you sometimes join in these girls' gossip and talk about Alicia behind her back.

☐ **b.** You don't start gossiping about Alicia, snubbing her, or taking sides against her. However, you don't stick up for her either. Sometimes, even though you don't take their side, the simple fact that you're with these girls makes it seem like you're against Alicia.

☐ **c.** You don't take these girls' side against Alicia. In fact, you stick up for Alicia.

9. You're at the shopping center with a bunch of your friends. You're in the makeup department and one of the girls takes a lipstick and puts it in her pocket. Everyone is kind of giggling and feeling all excited about what's going on. You've never shoplifted before and you don't want to start now. Your parents would hit the roof if you got caught shoplifting! But, the other girls are all doing it and they're urging you to do it too. "Come on, don't be such a baby," one girl says. You don't want to be a spoilsport or look like a chicken, but you're not too nuts about the idea of shoplifting either. If you were in this situation, what might you do?

☐ **a.** Shoplift something even though you don't really want to do it.

☐ **b.** Make up a quick excuse or a lie to get out of shoplifting. For example, you might say something like, "I don't have a pocket," or "Uh-oh! I think someone's coming!" or "We better get out of here. I think that lady saw us and she might be going to tell," or "There's nothing here I really want," or something along these lines.

☐ **c.** Say something like, "No way! If I got caught my parents would kill me!" or "You go ahead if you want to, but not me." "Are you guys nuts?

I'm not doing that" or "I wouldn't feel good about doing that," or simply "No." In any case, you make it clear to your friends that you're not going to shoplift no matter what they say or think.

10. A guy who's a couple of years older and a few grades ahead of you in school asks you to go a party. He's one of the neatest guys at your school, really good-looking. You can't believe this guy has even noticed you, much less asked you out! He runs around with an older and more sophisticated crowd and you're a little nervous about how you're supposed to act and what his friends will think of you. You don't want to come off like a kid! You get to the party and your date says, "What would you like to drink—a glass of wine, a beer?" Everyone at the party is under the drinking age, but everyone seems to be drinking alcohol of some kind. Your parents let you sip a beer or a glass of wine at home, but you'd be grounded forever if they knew you were drinking. Besides, you don't even like the taste of beer or wine. But your date seems to expect you to drink alcohol, and you don't want him to think you're some kind of goody-goody. If you were in this situation, what would you do?

   ☐ **a.** Go ahead and take a drink, even though you don't like the taste and don't feel good about drinking.

   ☐ **b.** Take a glass of beer or wine, but don't drink it. Just pretend to sip on it now and then to make it look like you're drinking without actually doing so.

   ☐ **c.** Say, "I'd rather have a coke," or "Thanks, I don't drink, I'll take a soda," or something along those lines. In any case, you make it clear that you'd prefer a non-alcoholic drink.

WHAT YOUR ANSWERS MEAN

Before we start, we want to make one thing very clear: Don't expect yourself to be an absolutely perfect person who doesn't give a hoot what others might do or say or think, never lets other people influence her thoughts or actions, and always does what she thinks is right, no matter what.

That's expecting too much of yourself. All of us human beings—whether we're little kids, preteens, teens, or full-grown adults—give into peer pressure now and then. Anybody who tries to tell you differently is a flat-out liar! So there's no use in getting down on yourself or kicking yourself in the behind because you've made a mistake or have given into peer pressure—all you'll get is a sore behind! Still, examining your responses in the situations here can help you find ways to follow your own true feelings and not just go along with the crowd.

As you may have guessed, an "a" answer means that you're really affected by peer pressure, at least in the kind of situation described.

A "b" answer means that, at least for that particular kind of situation, you're somewhat able to handle peer pressure. You don't give in to peer pressure all the way, but on the other hand, you don't really go with your true feelings either.

A "c" answer means that in the type of situation described, you do a very good job of handling peer pressure. You're able to go with your true feelings or your ideas of what's right for you without giving in to pressure from others.

Now that you have a general idea of what your answers mean, we'd like you to look back over your answers. Count up the number of "a," "b," and "c" answers and write your totals in the blanks below.

I had _____ "a" answers.
I had _____ "b" answers.
I had _____ "c" answers.

If you had 5 or more "a" answers: You are probably one of those people who is often kept from expressing her real feelings because of what others might think or do or say. You probably have trouble acting on your real feelings. You may be easily talked into doing (or not doing) something by others. You are easily influenced to act a certain way, even if you don't really want to.

You are also a very honest person. Although your "a" answers show that you often give in to peer pressure, at least you're able to admit this fact. This ability to be honest about yourself is very important. People often try to pretend that peer pressure doesn't affect them. We'd all like to think that we're strong enough or brave enough or whatever enough to stand up to peer pressure. But most of us, at least sometimes, have trouble with it. Admitting that you're affected by peer pressure is the first step in being able to change your reaction to it.

Begin by asking yourself if you *want* to change the way in which you handle peer pressure. Most kids who are affected by peer pressure do want to change. When we give into peer pressure, we go against our true feelings or our own ideas of what's right for us. Giving into peer pressure can make us feel just plain lousy about ourselves. At times, it can also get us into trouble. If, for example, giving into peer pressure means taking drugs, drinking, driving in a car with a teen driver who's been drinking, or something along these lines, then giving into peer pressure can have serious, even deadly, results.

If you would like to change the way you handle peer pressure, you can start by looking back over the ten situations in the quiz. Did you give "b" or "c" answers for any of the ten situations? If so, try to figure out what was different about those situations in which you gave a "b" or "c" answer. Why were you able to stand up to peer pressure in those particular situations instead of giving in? If you can figure out why peer pressure rules you in some situations and not in others, you'll have a better idea of your strengths and weaknesses when it comes to dealing with peer pressure.

If you have 5 or more "b" answers: You're not one of those people who totally goes her own way, completely follows her own feelings, or does only what she thinks is right, regardless of what others might do or say or think. But you're not a complete pushover either. You sometimes let peer pressure keep you from doing exactly what you may really think is right or from expressing your real feelings. But there's a point at which you draw the line.

Chances are that you are a very sensitive person. You're probably very aware of, or "tuned in" to, the thoughts and feelings of others. In fact, you're probably much more aware of others' thoughts and feelings than most people. On the one hand, your sensitivity to others is a good thing. It makes you a very caring person who is a good friend to others. On the other hand, your sensitivity to others may make you worry too much about being laughed at, teased, ridiculed or put down by others. As a result, you let peer pressure keep you from behaving in the way you'd really like to behave.

You're probably also the kind of person who goes out of her way to avoid fights, conflicts, and problems. Your way of dealing with problems and fights is to avoid them altogether. Rather than either giving in or actually facing up to and dealing with a problem or conflict, you figure out ways to get around the whole issue. Here again, in some ways, this is a good thing. You're able to make compromises, which allow you to avoid giving in to peer pressure all the way. But, by going around problems instead of facing up to them, you may sometimes run into trouble. You may compromise too much when it comes to peer pressure. You may end up feeling not-so-great about yourself or even getting into trouble.

If you had 5 or more "b" answers, look back over the situations in which you gave "b" answers. Then ask yourself this question: Would I have felt better, been happier with myself, or felt prouder if I had been able to give a "c" answer instead of a "b" answer? If you had one or more "c" answers, ask yourself this question: Do I feel better about myself in those situations in which I gave "c" answers? If the answer to either of these questions is "yes," be sure to read the section, "How to Handle Peer Pressure."

If you had 5 or more "c" answers: Congratulations! You are one of those rare people who is able to stand up to peer pressure very well. If *all* ten of your answers were "c's," you can give yourself a pat on the back. You're a regular Superwoman when it comes to handling peer pressure!

Having 5 or more "c" answers shows that you are a very self-confident person who probably feels very good about herself. Chances are that you're not easily talked into doing or saying something that doesn't seem right to you. You're usually not afraid to take an unpopular stand or to express your real feelings and act on them, regardless of what others might say or do. You don't often let your peers make your decisions for you.

Kids like you are sometimes the "leaders" of their group or crowd. Other kids often admire and respect you because you're able to stick by your convictions and go with your true feelings. But life isn't always a bed of roses for someone like you. Sometimes it can be pretty difficult. As you probably know, standing up to peer pressure doesn't always mean that everyone is going to admire and respect you. In fact, sometimes people may ridicule, tease, or put you down because you refuse to give into peer pressure. You may lose "popularity points" for refusing to give into peer pressure. Although you have the inner strength to stand up for your own ideas of what's right, you may have times when you feel lonely or out of it. If so, hang in there. In the long run, we think that you'll be glad you did.

But if you do find that standing up to peer pressure makes you unpopular, you might want to think a bit more carefully about exactly how you handle peer pressure. Now, don't get us wrong! We're not suggesting that you start giving in to peer pressure in order to get other people to like you better. No way! But, sometimes, without even meaning to, people can end up sounding like they're preaching to others or like they're looking down their nose at them because they do give into peer pressure. There are ways of saying no and not giving into peer pressure without putting others down. If you think that it would help you to be a bit more tactful or polite or gentle in terms of the way you say no to peer pressure, be sure to read the section "How to Handle Peer Pressure."

If most of your answers were "c's," but some were "a's" or "b's," you might want to think about those situations in which you gave an "a" or "b" answer. Why were those situations different from the ones for which you gave a "c" answer? What was it about those situations that would cause you to give into peer pressure, instead of standing up to it as you usually do? By answering these two questions, you'll have a better idea of your strong points and your weak points when it comes to peer pressure.

If you didn't have 5 or more answers that were the same: You're one of those people who handles peer pressure in a variety of different ways. In some situations, you probably do pretty well; in others, not so well.

You might want to read what we've written above for people who had mostly "a," "b," and "c" answers. Chances are that some of the things we've said to those people will hold true for you, too. You might also look over the ten situations in the above quiz again and ask yourself why you gave different answers for different situations. What was it about one situation that made you give a "c" or "b" answer, while for others you gave an "a"? If you can figure out the answers to these questions, you'll know more about your strength and weakness when it comes to dealing with peer pressure.

Also, ask yourself these questions: Am I happy with the answers I gave? Would I have felt better about myself if I'd been able to give a "c" answer instead of an "a" or "b" answer? If the answers to either or both of these questions is yes, be sure to read the section "How to Handle Peer Pressure."

How to Handle Peer Pressure

Peer pressure isn't an easy thing to handle, and there just aren't any simple, "one-two-three-and-you're-home-free" ways of dealing with it. But we think the suggestions, advice, and tips listed below may help you to handle peer pressure a bit better.

The suggestions below aren't foolproof. They won't work in every situation. But these tips have helped others, and so we'd like you to read through the list and think about this advice. If something on the list sounds like it might be helpful to you or worth remembering, you should put a check mark in the appropriate box.

☐ **1.** *Think Ahead!*

One thing that's helpful for many people is to think ahead. Ask yourself these kinds of questions: What might happen if I do give in to or go along with peer pressure? What might happen if I don't? How will I feel about myself afterward? How might other people react to me if I do, or if I don't, give in? Could I get into trouble if I do go along with peer pressure? What will it "cost" me not to go along or give in or to stand up to peer pressure? What will it "cost" me if I do? Am I willing to "pay" the possible price?

Suppose, for example, that you're in a situation where kids are passing around a joint (a marijuana cigarette). What might happen if you did smoke?

- You might get caught and get in trouble with your parents or with the police.
- You might cough and look stupid.
- You might wish you hadn't or be down on yourself for giving in.
- You might like it and be taking the first step on the road to becoming a drug user.
- The other kids might think you're cool and might accept you into their group more.

What might happen if you *don't* smoke?

- The other kids might make fun of you, call you a chicken, put you down, tease you, or give you a hard time.
- The other kids might not feel so friendly toward you anymore, or they might not want you around if you won't do what they do.
- The other kids might admire or respect you, or someone else who really doesn't want to do it may follow your example and say "no" too.
- The other kids might learn that you can still be their friend even if you don't do what they do.

Of course, when you're in a peer pressure situation, you often have to make a decision right away, right there, on the spot. You may not have a lot of time. Still, you can usually manage to take just a few seconds to think ahead to what the results of your decision might be, and it's usually worthwhile to do so.

However, we don't want to kid you. Even if you do manage to think ahead, this doesn't necessarily mean that you'll know exactly what to do or that you'll make the right decision for you. In fact, in some situations, thinking about all the things that might happen can make it all the more confusing or harder for you to decide what to do. But, the fact that you've thought ahead gives you a better chance of doing what's right for you. And, if you've thought ahead, you're much less likely to be caught off guard or to be surprised by whatever does happen.

☐ **2.** *Talk Honestly About Your Feelings and Invite Others to Do the Same.*

If you really don't feel okay about whatever is happening, if you think it's just not right, or if you're going to feel crummy about yourself because you gave in or didn't stand up to peer pressure, you can be honest about your feelings. Saying something along these lines is often helpful:

- "I don't feel good about this."
- "I'd feel really lousy about doing that."
- "I don't feel comfortable doing this."
- "I know I'll feel crummy about myself afterward."
- "If I do, I know I'll be sorry later."
- "I just don't think this is the right thing to do."

Other people respect people who respect themselves and have the guts to say what they're really feeling. Sometimes just being honest about your feelings is enough to get you out of a sticky situation.

A lot of times, the other kids involved in the situation may share your feelings. Once you've been honest about your feelings, some of them may find it easier to talk honestly about their feelings. You can even invite them to do so. Of course, you don't want to say something totally dumb like "Could you tell me what your honest feelings are about this situation?" But you could say something along these lines:

- "Gee, I'm not too nuts about this idea, what do you think?"
- "To tell you the truth I feel real weird about this. What do you think?"
- "You know, when I'm in a situation like this, I sometimes feel _____" (Fill in the blank with an explanation of how you feel.) "Do you ever feel that way?"

Here again, this isn't a 100%, foolproof way of handling peer pressure. But, people often respect people who are able to be honest, and they're often grateful when someone else helps them have a chance to be honest about their own feelings.

☐ **3.** *Use Humor and Exaggeration.*
Many times we find ourselves in a peer pressure situation when we want to say no or to stand up to the rest of the group. However, we don't always know how to do this without sounding like a goody-goody. One way of handling these situations is to use a little humor and exaggeration. Here are some examples of ways in which you can use humor and exaggeration in dealing with peer pressure situations:

- You think that whatever you're feeling pressured to do could be an unwise, or even a dangerous thing to do. Instead of merely saying that it's dangerous, unwise or whatever, use exaggeration to get your point across: "Are you nuts? That's the stupidest, craziest idea I ever heard!" Or, "You guys need your heads examined! What you're doing isn't just dumb, it's totally insane." Or, "Hey, why bother doing that? Why go to all that trouble! Why don't we just go out and get a gun and shoot ourselves in the head?"
- You think that what you're being pressured to do is morally wrong, dishonest or unethical. You can get your point across and avoid preaching or sound-

ing like a Sunday School teacher by using humorous exaggeration: "No way am I gonna do that! Not only is it wrong [dishonest, unethical or whatever], it's completely low-life." Or, "What is it with you guys? Are you trying out for the scumbag-of-the-universe award? I can't believe you're actually [suggesting whatever they're suggesting, saying whatever they're saying, doing whatever they're doing]."

• You're worried about what might happen if you give in or go along. Don't just admit you're worried or concerned, exaggerate your worry in a funny way: "I'm afraid that if I cheat, I'll get caught and shipped off to Siberia." Or, "If I smoke this cigarette, I'm afraid I'll throw up all over the place and probably all over you, too!"

• You're afraid that your friends will react to you in a negative way. Exaggerate their possible reactions: "If I join the debate club, I'm afraid you'll put me up for membership in the Nerd-of-the-Month Club." Or, "If I stick up for so and so, I'm afraid you'll all think I'm the biggest jerk that ever walked the face of the earth."

• You're stuck or uncertain about what to do. Don't merely say you're stuck, exaggerate how stuck you're feeling: "I think I'm about to go crazy here. I want to and I don't want to. I feel like a train trying to go in two different directions at once."

We could go on and on giving you examples of how humor and exaggeration can help you deal with peer pressure situations. But, we think you've got the idea. So, why not try it out the next time you find yourself having to deal with peer pressure?

☐ **4.** *Use Parents As An Excuse.*

Parents can sometimes be a drag, but they can also be very useful, especially when it comes to dealing with peer pressure. If, for example, you're in a peer pressure situation and you don't quite know how to say no, why not use your parents as an excuse? Saying something like: "My parents won't let me," "I promised my parents I wouldn't"; or "My parents would kill me" can sometimes get you out of a sticky situation. Your friends will often get off your case, or at least be very understanding about why you're not going along with them if you use your parents as an excuse. After all, everyone knows how terrible and unreasonable parents can be!

This isn't, of course, a foolproof scheme for dealing with peer pressure. In fact, in some cases, the last thing you want to do is to admit that you're worried about what your parents might think or do! If so, it might help if you combine humor and exaggeration along with using your parents as an excuse. You might, for instance, say something along these lines:

• "Are you kidding? If I did that my parents would hang me up by my heels from the living-room ceiling."

• "If I got caught, my parents would take me out in the back yard and shoot me!"

• "Oh sure! You get caught and maybe your parents will ground you for a couple of days or cut off your allowance for a week. I get caught, and with my parents, it'd be World War III!"

• "Hey, I'd like to, but you don't know my parents. I swear they've got eyes in the back of their heads! They can smell it when I do something wrong. Really, they should work for the CIA!"

• "Easy for you to say, 'So what if we do get caught!' Your parents are reasonable human beings. My parents think Attila the Hun was a nice guy. They find out, and I'm grounded forever or maybe even shipped off to a nunnery!"

• "Yeah, you're good at pulling the wool over your parents' eyes. But, I'm not. My parents have a built-in radar system. They *always* find out."

Of course, there are very few parents who have eyes in back of their heads or a built-in radar system. And, there are very few parents who would actually hang their kid up by her heels from the living-room ceiling or take her out in the back yard and shoot her, no matter what she may have done. But, by combining humor and exaggeration along with using your parents as an excuse, you can often get yourself out of a tough situation.

☐ **5.** *Just Say "No."*

There is one absolutely foolproof way of dealing with peer pressure: Just say no. And, sometimes, that is all you can do. It isn't always easy to say no, but when the going gets tough, it's often the best choice.

INTERVIEW

We've given you some of our suggestions and tips on how to handle peer pressure, but it might also be helpful for you to hear about someone else's experiences and advice. Why not try interviewing one of your parents or another adult you know and respect to find out how they handle peer pressure? Explain that you've been thinking about peer pressure and that you'd like to know what they think also. Below is a list of questions you might ask:

1. When you were my age did you ever have a situation in which you gave in to peer pressure? Describe the situation and explain why you gave in. _____

_____

_____

_____

_____

2. What happened because you gave in or went along? Were you happy with the results? How did you feel about yourself afterwards? How did others react?

Did you get in trouble or have any problems as a result of giving in or going along?

_____

_____

_____

3. Do you wish that you'd handled the situation any differently? Or, now that you're older, can you think of any ways in which you could have handled the situation differently?

_____

_____

_____

4. When you were my age did you ever have a situation in which you stood up to peer pressure or refused to give in or go along? Describe the situation and explain why you decided not to give in or go along.

_____

_____

_____

5. What happened because you didn't give in? How did you feel about yourself? How did others react? What did it "cost" you to stand up to peer pressure?

_____

_____

_____

6. Give me an example of a situation that's happened to you as an adult in which you gave in to peer pressure. Describe what happened, why you gave in, and how you felt about it afterwards. Do you wish you'd done something differently? If so, what?_____

_____

_____

_____

7. Give me an example of a situation you've faced as an adult in which you didn't give in to peer pressure. Describe what happened, why you didn't give in, and how you felt afterwards.

_____

_____

_____

8. Why do you think that you give in to peer pressure sometimes, but not at other times? What's the difference between those kinds of situations in which you let peer pressure get to you and those situations in which you don't?

_____

_____

_____

9. Here's an example of a peer pressure situation that's come up in my life (give an example). If you were me how might you handle this situation?_____

_____

_____

_____

4: CRUSHES AND BOY/GIRL RELATIONSHIPS

Having a crush means having romantic or sexual feelings for another person. As we go through puberty and adolescence, many of us develop crushes. Of course, some of us have crushes long before puberty and adolescence and some of us don't develop crushes until we're older. But for many of us the preteen or teen years are when we first begin to have serious crushes. In this chapter we'll be talking about crushes, and asking you to write about your answers.

We'll also be talking about boy/girl relationships. During the preteen and teen years, many girls begin dating or start having boyfriends. Having a romance can be exciting, but it can also cause problems or raise questions in our lives. This chapter will help you find solutions to your problems, and answers to your questions.

Having a crush can be very exciting. Just thinking about or catching sight of the person we have a crush on can brighten our whole day. We may spend many happy hours thinking about that special someone. But having a crush can also cause problems, especially if the person we have a crush on doesn't return our feelings.

We asked the boys and girls and men and women we talked with to tell us about their experiences with crushes. In the next few pages, we'll be letting you know what some of the people had to say about crushes, and asking you to write about your feelings about crushes that you or your friends may have had in the past or may be having right now.

Same-Sex Crushes

One of the interesting things we learned from talking to people about crushes is that many, many young people develop crushes on someone who is the same sex as they are. A number of the people we talked to, both males and females, told us about having romantic or sexual feelings toward someone of the same sex. One woman had this to say:

> *When I was about eleven years old, I had a crush on my homeroom teacher. She was very pretty and very kind, and I had very strong feelings about her. I'd hang around after school, offering to wash the blackboards and correct papers for her. I'd have done anything for her! Just a smile or a kind word from her would have me on cloud nine.*

Another woman told us that she'd had a crush on her girlfriend when the two of them were eleven:

> *We were the best of friends. And we were also a bit in love with each other. We'd hug and kiss and we had this great plan that we were going to grow up and live together, as if we were going to marry each other.*

Like all crushes, same-sex crushes can be fun and exciting and are a special way of experimenting with our romantic and sexual feelings. Many young people have same-sex crushes or experiences. In fact, it is very common and not at all unusual.

Some of the people we talked to were uncomfortable about the fact that they had same-sex crushes. Some wondered if it was "normal" to have romantic or sexual feelings about someone of the same sex. Others worried that they were "weird" or that there was "something wrong" with them because they had these sorts of feelings. If you've worried about this, you can relax. Having same-sex crushes doesn't mean there's anything wrong with you or weird about you. It's perfectly normal, perfectly natural, and perfectly okay.

"Star" Crushes

In addition to telling us about same-sex crushes, many of the people we talked to told us about having crushes on a "star"— on an actor or actress, on a rock and role musician or singer, or on some other famous person whom they'd never actually met and probably never would meet.

Of course, not everyone gets these crushes, but most people we talked to at least knew someone who did. Some people thought having a star crush was okay or even a good thing. Some didn't really have a strong opinion one way or the other. But, some people thought having star crushes was silly or downright stupid. One girl had this to say:

My friends all have crushes on rock stars or actors or someone like that.
I think it's stupid . . . a real waste of time. I just can't get into it. I mean
really . . . like they're ever going to even see this person! If they did,
they'd be so tongue-tied, they won't be able to talk to 'em. It kind of em-
barrasses me how they go on and on . . . I feel kind of out of it some-
times because they say, "Oh don't you just love him." I don't "just love"
him, and neither do they really. Sometimes, I'll act like I really think
this star is great big deal, but really it just seems stupid to me. I wish
they wouldn't act so dumb about it . . . I don't know how to act when
they get into it.

For people who do get star crushes, their feelings can just be mild ones—enjoying daydreaming about the star from time to time and imagining what it would be like to be with such a glamorous, famous person. Or this kind of crush can be very strong, so that the person who has the crush spends a lot of time and energy thinking and daydreaming about the star. For instance, one girl we know had a very strong crush on Michael Jackson when she was thirteen. Her bedroom wall was plastered with Michael Jackson posters. She had every record of his and listened to them over and over again. She also had stacks of fan magazines with articles about him, which she read and reread. She belonged to a Michael Jackson fan club. She and her girlfriends, who also had crushes on Michael Jackson, would spend hours talking about him. In short, the girl had a serious crush!

Now that she's older (she's sixteen now), this girl is not so interested in Michael Jackson. She's much more interested in her real-life boyfriend, a boy her own age whom she met at school. But, for a time, when she was thirteen, Michael Jackson seemed to be the main interest in her life.

Having a star crush, whether it's a mild crush or a very strong one, can be fun. Collecting pictures of the star, watching the star on television or in the movies, reading about the star, sharing our feelings with friends who also have crushes on the star can help make our crushes even more exciting. And, this kind of crush can be a healthy way of "trying out," or experimenting with, our romantic and sexual feelings.

A star crush is also nice because it's "safe." A star crush is safe because, even though we may pretend a lot, somewhere deep inside, we know that we're never really going to meet the star. When we have real-life crushes on people we actually know, we have to worry about all sorts of real-life problems: about whether or not that person will like us back; about being rejected or "put down" or risking getting our feelings hurt; about how we should act or what we should say to that real-life person. But, when we have star crushes, we don't have to worry about any of these things. We're in control! Since we're making it all up, we can imagine things turning out the way we'd like!

The only problem with star crushes is that sometimes we can get too carried away. For example, one year, a group of girls developed a crush on a famous young actor/singer. They papered their bedroom walls with his posters, wore buttons with his face printed on them, wrote fan letters, and had a great time oohing and aahing over him. When the star got married, they were, of course, a little bit let down, but one girl was actually miserable. She had gotten so involved in her crush that, in her mind, it was as if she was really in love with the star. His marriage seemed like the end of the world to her.

If you develop a serious star crush, it helps to remind yourself from time to time that your crush isn't very realistic and that it's unlikely that the star will ever meet you and fall in love with you. This isn't to say that you should give up your crush or try to forget about this wonderful, unattainable person. You shouldn't. Star crushes are, as we've said, an important way of experimenting with our romantic and sexual feelings. But do remind yourself from time to time that your crush is just a fantasy and that it's really not very likely that you and your star crush will ever really meet and get to know each other.

Crushes on Someone Older

Some people told us about having crushes on a teacher, on another adult, on the friend of an older brother or sister, or on some other person who was so much older than they were that it was unlikely that the person would ever return their feelings, simply because of the difference in ages. Like "star" crushes, crushes on someone older can be fun and exciting. They are also "safe" crushes because much as we may pretend otherwise, some part of us knows that this older person won't really like us back, at least not in the romantic or sexual way that we like them. Because we know this, we're free to enjoy our fantasy without having to worry about what would happen if that person really returned our feelings. These kinds of crushes are, then, a safe way of experimenting with our romantic and sexual feelings before we get into a real-life relationship with someone more our own age.

The only problem with crushes on someone older is that, like star crushes, these crushes can get out of hand. If we get too involved in our pretending, we may forget that, because of the age differences, it's really not very likely that this person will return our feelings. For instance, one girl, whom we'll call Sally, wrote to us:

> *I have a crush on my teacher at school. I dream about him all the time, especially at night. I sometimes feel like he's really there, and we're talking about getting married and having babies! What should I do? Sometimes I think he really loves me because he wrote me a note that said, "Love, Mr. P.!" Plus he always smiles at me in a really funny way, like he loves me! I don't know what to do about it.*

If, like this girl, you've had or are having a crush on an older person, you might want to read part of the letter we wrote back to this girl, which is reprinted here:

> *It's quite normal for a girl your age to have a crush on her teacher. It's also normal to have these kinds of fantasies, daydreams and night dreams*

about the person you have a crush on. In fact, it's a sign that you are growing up! All these fantasies are a sort of rehearsal, a way of practicing, for someday when you will really get married and really have babies with someone of your own age. In fact, I think crushes are some of the nicest feelings we can have. I hope you'll enjoy your crush on Mr. P.

The only problem I see with crushes is that sometimes when we get crushes on people, we get too wrapped up in our crushes. We may begin to hope that the person we have a crush on will feel the same way about us. When we realize that person doesn't, we can get to feeling awfully sad and blue.

I think it's very important for you to have your crush on Mr. P. But, I think it's important not to get things mixed up. You have to remember that Mr. P is a grown-up man. His romantic feelings are always going to be about someone his own age, not someone your age. I'll bet you're someone very special to him. Maybe even the teacher's pet. But, when he signed the note, "Love, Mr. P," I'm sure he meant "love" in a different way than you are hoping he meant love.

Still, fantasies and crushes are an important part of our lives, and I hope you enjoy yours.

FREEWRITING EXERCISE

Have you ever had a crush on a girlfriend? Or on a star, or teacher? On another adult, friend of an older brother or sister, or on some other person older than you? Or, do you know someone who's had one of these sorts of crushes? Use the space below to freewrite about your crush, about a crush a friend of yours may have had, or just about your feelings about those kinds of crushes.

_____

_____

_____

_____

_____

_____

_____

_____

_____

_____

_____

Not-So-Impossible Crushes

"Star" crushes and crushes on someone older are, in a sense, "impossible" crushes because it's just not very likely that the person you have a crush on will ever return your feelings. But not all crushes are "impossible." In fact, most people eventually get crushes on someone that they actually know (or have at least met), someone about their own age, who might possibly return their feelings.

Some girls told us they don't really like having people use the word "crush" to describe their feelings. One girl put it this way:

> *I hate that word "crush," like when parents say, "Oh, she has a crush on him! Isn't that cute!" It sounds so stupid, like you're this lovesick dog, all hung-up and moony-eyed over someone. . . . It's like they're teasing you about your feelings and putting you down.*

Another girl said:

> *"Crush" isn't a good word. It makes it sound like this great big deal. There's this certain boy that I like a lot, and I think maybe he likes me too. But I don't have this giant crush on him. I just like him is all.*

And maybe these girls are right. Perhaps *crush* isn't really a good word for describing these not-so-impossible romantic attractions. But, whether you call it a "crush" or just "liking someone," the fact of the matter is that many of us do become romantically attracted to a certain special someone during our preteen or teen years. How about you? Is there someone special in your life? Or, if there isn't someone special right now, has there been in the past? If so, we'd like you to use the blank space below to freewrite about that person. (If you've never had a crush or been interested in someone, wait until this does happen and come back and write about it.)

You might tell that person's name, how you met, what attracted you to that person, whether or not that person returned your feelings, and any other details you want to include. Just think about that person and start writing. Don't stop until you've filled up all the blank spaces.

_____

_____

_____

_____

_____

_____

_____

_____

_____

_____

_____

Boy-Girl Relationships

During the preteen and teen years of puberty and adolescence, there may be many important "firsts" in our lives: first serious crush; first real boyfriend; first date; first kiss; first true love; and so on. These new developments in our romantic lives can be very exciting, but they can also make our lives more complicated than when we were younger. Once you or the other kids your age are bitten by the 'ole love bug, your life and your relationship with others usually begins to change in many important ways. These changes can, as we've said, be very exciting, but they're often a mixed bag. These changes may create difficulties or cause problems in our lives. We may find ourselves faced with questions that we've never had to think about before. We may not know just how to answer these questions.

Over the years, the boys and girls in our classes, the readers who've written to us, and the people we've interviewed have told us about the problems and difficulties that they had to face once the love bug began biting them or the other kids their age. They also asked a lot of questions. And, by "a lot," we mean *a lot*! It would take another whole book just to list them all.

There's just no way we'll be able to get all these questions in this book; however, we would like to share at least some of them with you. You may find some of these same questions popping up in your own life.

Below is a list of some of the questions we've been asked over the years. We'd like you to read through the list. If one of the questions on the list sounds familiar to you, we'd like you to put a check mark in the box in front of that question. In other words, if the question sounds like one you've had or something you've wondered about, check the box in front of that question. Then, when you're finished doing that, we'd like you to do the exercise that follows.

QUESTIONS

☐ **1.** Is it normal for a girl my age to spend so much time thinking, dreaming, or fantasizing about boys and things like romance, love, marriage, or sex?

☐ **2.** Is there something wrong with you if the other girls your age are interested in boys, but you just aren't interested in boys in "that way" or don't feel ready for things like dating or having a boyfriend yet?

☐ **3.** What if you feel left out because your friends have boyfriends and you don't? Should you get involved with a boy you don't really like just so you, too, will have a boyfriend?

☐ **4.** Suppose that you'd like to have a boyfriend, but you've never had one and you're beginning to wonder if you ever will?

☐ **5.** How do you let a boy know that you like him? How can you find out if he likes you?

☐ **6.** What should you do if someone likes you, but you're not interested in him, at least not in a romantic way?

☐ **7.** Is it all right for a girl to ask a boy out?

☐ **8.** What if you and your girlfriend like the same boy?

☐ **9.** Suppose you've been good friends with a boy, but you want to be more than just friends with him?

☐ **10.** What if you like a boy, but none of your friends likes him and they're always putting him down?

☐ **11.** What if you like two boys and you can't decide which one you like best? Is it okay to have more than one boyfriend at a time?

☐ **12.** Suppose you want to date or have a boyfriend, but your parents say "no way"?

☐ **13.** How do you know if you're really in love?

☐ **14.** How can you break up with your boyfriend without hurting his feelings?

EXERCISE

Have you ever read "Dear Abby," "Dear Ann Landers," or one of the other advice columns in the newspaper? Well, in this exercise, you're going to ask someone to be your own personal advice columnist.

The exercise, which has four steps, will help you find answers to the questions in the list above.

Step One: In order to do this exercise, you first need to choose four questions from the list. Pick questions that are most interesting or most important to you. It would probably be best if you choose questions that you put a check mark in front of when you first read through the list, but any four questions will do.

Then, you'll need to copy the four questions you've chosen into the boxes A through D that follow. It doesn't matter which questions you write in which box. Just write one question in box A, one in box B, and so on until you've copied each of your four questions into one of the boxes.

You may need to write smaller than you usually do in order to fit the entire question in the box. It will be helpful for you to know the number of the question later on in this exercise, so copy the question's number from the list as well as the question itself.

After you've copied the questions into the boxes, do Step Two, which follows them.

BOX A:

BOX B:

BOX C:

BOX D:

```
┌─────────────────────────────────────────────────────────┐
│                                                         │
├─────────────────────────────────────────────────────────┤
│                                                         │
└─────────────────────────────────────────────────────────┘
```

_____

_____

_____

_____

Step Two: For this step you'll need to find a partner, someone who'll act as an advice columnist for you. Ask someone you trust and feel comfortable with, and choose someone whose opinions you respect and who'll be able to give you good advice. You might want to ask your mom, your dad, another relative, another adult, or a close friend. It would probably be best if you asked someone who's older than you and who may know more about life than you, but it's also okay to choose someone your own age.

Show your partner the four questions you've copied into boxes A, B, C, and D. Explain that you want your partner to read each of the questions and write his or her answers in the spaces below each box.

Explain to your partner that things like spelling, grammar, or punctuation aren't so important, and that it's perfectly fine to use simple, short phrases instead of complete sentences. After all, this isn't an English essay or a home-work assignment! But, do ask your partner to think carefully before answering.

Once your partner has finished writing his or her answers, have your partner read, and if necessary, explain all four answers. After you've done this, you're ready for Step Three.

Step Three: We have written answers for all of the questions that began on page 59. Our answers begin on page 64. We'd now like you to turn to those pages and find our answers to the four questions you've been using in this exercise. You and your partner should read our answers and discuss them.

You may find that your partner's answers are nearly the same as ours, or you may find that your partner's answers are very different. In any case, ask your partner to tell you what she or he thinks of our answers.

Once you've done this, you're ready for Step Four. You won't need your partner for Step Four. But, don't forget to thank your partner for helping you before you move on to this step.

Step Four: As we say, your partner's answers may have been very similar to our answers, or your partner's answers may have been quite different or even opposite from yours. Actually, it's not so important whether the answers were the same or different. What's important is that, in doing this exercise, you've gotten two answers, one from your partner and one from us.

When we have questions that we don't quite know how to answer, it's often helpful to get opinions from one or more other people, and that's what you've been doing in this exercise. Now that you've gotten a couple of opinions, we'd like you to answer those questions for yourself.

In the spaces below, write your answers to the four questions you've been using in this exercise. You don't have to use complete sentences or worry about grammar. If you'd like, you can just freewrite your answer.

Question A: _____

_____

_____

_____

_____

Question B: _____

_____

_____

_____

_____

Question C: _____

_____

_____

_____

_____

Question D: _____

_____

_____

_____

_____

If this exercise has been helpful to you, you might want to try it again using other questions and/or other partners. Of course, you've already filled up the boxes in this book and your partner has already written in the blank spaces below the questions, but you can just use any blank sheet of paper if you want to do the exercise again. Simply write your question at the top of the paper and let your partner use the rest of the space to write his or her answer. After you've compared your partner's answer with ours, you can write your answer on the back of the paper or on a separate sheet.

(P.S.: If you do decide to try the exercise again, be sure to save the papers you've used to write the questions and answers. Fold them up and tuck them inside the book. You'll get a big kick out of reading them again when you're older. And, if you someday become the mother of a girl child and you pass this book on to her, we promise you that she'll get a kick out of reading whatever you've written.)

1. *Is it normal for a girl my age to spend so much time thinking, dreaming, or fantasizing about boys, and things like romance, love, marriage, or sex?*

Yes, it's perfectly normal and natural for a girl to spend a lot of time, even a *whole lot* of time, thinking, dreaming, or fantasizing about such things. Of course, not all girls spend their time this way, but many preteen and teenage girls do.

Sometimes a girl worries because she thinks her thoughts, dreams, or fantasies are "too silly," "too weird," or "too far-out." But, you really needn't worry about this. All of us have silly, weird, or far-out thoughts, dreams, or fantasies from time to time. It's perfectly normal!

At other times, a girl worries that she's too "boy-crazy" or that she's spending too much time fantasizing. But, unless you're spending nearly all your waking hours thinking about these things or unless your fantasies start to seem more real than the rest of your life, you needn't really worry. If, however, you are spending nearly all your waking hours fantasizing, if your fantasies become more real than the rest of your life, or if something about your fantasies bothers you, you should talk to someone about this. See pages 145–152 for suggestions about who you might talk to. Other than this, though, you can feel free to relax and enjoy yourself, knowing that this sort of thinking, daydreaming, and fantasizing is perfectly normal for a girl your age.

2. *Is there something wrong with you if the other girls your age are interested in boys, but you just aren't interested in boys in "that way" or don't feel ready for things like dating or having a boyfriend yet?*

If you're worried about something like this, you can relax. There's nothing wrong with you! Just as we each have our own personal timetables of development when it comes to the physical body changes of puberty, so we each have our own personal timetables when it comes to romantic matters. Some of us get interested in boys and in things like dating when we're still fairly young. Others don't get interested in or feel ready for these things until we're older. If the other girls your age are interested in romance and you're not, this doesn't mean that there's something wrong with you. It just means that your timetable is slower than the other girls'. There's nothing wrong with being slower. It's just slower— that's all. So, relax, enjoy life, and know that, sooner or later, romance *will* be a part of your life.

3. *What if you feel left out because your friends have boyfriends and you don't? Should you get involved with a boy you don't really like just so you, too, will have a boyfriend?*

Not having a boyfriend when most of your girlfriends do can make you feel awfully out of it. Sometimes, a girl gets to feeling that she should pair up with any 'ole boy who seems willing to be her boyfriend, even if she doesn't really like that boy, just so she won't feel left out. If you get to feeling this way, you need to think carefully before you get involved with "just anybody," simply for the sake of having someone to call your boyfriend. Is it really worth being paired up with someone you don't truly like just so you won't feel left out? Do you really need a boyfriend in order to feel good about yourself around your friends? Is it really fair to a boy to get involved with him if you don't really like him as a boyfriend?

Instead of getting involved with someone you don't really like, you might decide to make new friends or to spend more time with girls who don't have boyfriends, at least until you do find a boyfriend you really like or until they break up with their boyfriends. Or, you could decide to go along anyhow when your girlfriends and their boyfriends are doing things like going to parties, dances, or the movies or when they're going places as couples, even though you don't have a boyfriend. Or, perhaps you could ask a boy that you're "just friends" with to come along and be your partner in these sorts of situations.

Most important, remember that it's not a boyfriend that makes you a special person; it's being who you are. With or without a boyfriend, you're still the same, special person.

4. *Suppose that you'd like to have a boyfriend, but you've never had one and you're beginning to wonder if you ever will?*

If the other girls you know have already started dating or having boyfriends, but you haven't, you may get to feeling that these things won't ever happen to you. If so, it helps to remember that, sooner or later, you *will* find someone special. People always do! It also helps to remember that, just as we each have our own special timetable of development when it comes to the physical body changes of puberty, so we each have our own timetables when it comes to romantic matters. It can be awfully hard on us if our personal timetable is moving along more slowly than the other girls'. But, the fact that we're getting a slow start as far as dating or having a boyfriend goes doesn't mean that we won't ever start doing these things. It may take a while, but eventually these things will happen for you. We guarantee it!

Remember, too, that you've got a lot of years ahead of you. In the long run, it doesn't really matter if you've found your first boyfriend when you're only ten or not until you're twenty. What's important in the long run is that you feel good about yourself, so don't let the fact that romance isn't yet a part of your life get you down or make you feel bad about yourself.

5. *How do you let a boy know that you like him? How do you find out if he likes you?*

There are basically two answers to these questions: You can do it on your own, or you can have a friend do it for you.

If you decide to have a friend do it, be sure to pick a friend you can really trust, or next thing you know, it will be all over the school! It's often easier to let someone else do the talking for you, but keep in mind that, if you do this, you don't have very much control over what's being said. Suppose, for example, you only want your friend to bring up your name in a roundabout way and see how he reacts. Your friend may not do it exactly the way you'd like her to; instead, she might tell him that you're madly in love with him!

For these reasons, many girls prefer doing it on their own. You can let a boy know you like him by being friendly, starting conversations, going out of your way to be around him, asking him to go out with you, showing him how you feel by the way you act, or simply telling him how you feel. You can find out if he likes you by watching to see if he does any of these sorts of things to you.

Regardless of whether you tell a boy you like him yourself or have a friend do it for you, make sure it's done in private and not in front of the other kids. The boy may be so embarrassed if it's done in front of other kids that he may say he doesn't like you even if he really does. He may even stop liking you if you embarrass him in this way, so it's best to do it in private.

6. *What should you do if someone likes you, but you're not interested in him, at least not in a romantic way?*

Our basic rule here is: be honest, but be kind! It's usually a good idea to be as considerate and as nice as possible in letting him know you're just not interested in him. Not only is it kinder to him, but other people will probably respect you for being kind.

The exact way in which you handle this situation will usually depend on just how you've found out that he likes you. If he's gotten someone else to tell you how he feels, you can simply tell that person you're not interested in him. You might also say something nice about him, so he won't feel so bad; at least, don't

say anything unkind. You're not going to gain anything by saying something like, "Ugh, him! Are you kidding?" And, he'll probably feel really hurt if he hears what you've said. Even if you don't care about hurting his feelings, remember that another boy whom you do like may hear about your unkindness and may be afraid to tell you about his feelings for you.

If a boy tells you that he likes you directly—by writing you a note or by telling you so—it's best to let him know you're not interested yourself, rather than having someone else do it for you. It's also best to tell him in private rather than telling him in front of other kids. You might say something like, "I really think you're terrific and I really like you for a friend, but I'm just not interested in you as a boyfriend," or "I'm sorry, but I already have a boyfriend," or "I'm really flattered that you like me, but I just don't feel the same way about you," or something else along these lines.

7. *Is it all right for a girl to ask a boy out?*
Back in your parents' day, this was a definite no-no. Of course, even back then, there were some brave girls who went ahead and asked the boys out. And, most girls did everything they could, short of actually asking, in order to get the boys they liked to ask them out. But, the "rules" that most people went by said that boys did the asking and girls were supposed to wait to be asked.

Nowadays things have changed. Although there are still some people who think it's not "right" or "proper" for girls to do the asking, most people don't see anything at all wrong with it. In fact, many people think it's a great idea. Almost every boy we've ever asked has said he wished more girls would do it. Girls are usually in favor of it too. However, many girls have also admitted to being so worried about what others might think or so afraid that the boy might say no, that they can't really bring themselves to actually ask a boy out.

Our opinion: Go for it! If you're interested in someone, ask him out. After all, the worst that could happen is that he'll say no. That wouldn't really be the end of the world, would it? No one's ever died from being turned down for a date. Besides, if you wait to be asked, you may never be asked. As one girl put it, "My boyfriend's so shy. We'd never have gotten together if I hadn't gotten the ball rolling by asking him out. I'm glad I did!"

8. *What if you and your best friend like the same boy?*
If one of you is already dating or going with this boy, then we'd say that this boy was "off limits." But, if he's not "taken," then the two of you need to think about how you're going to keep youir feelings for this boy from getting in the way of, or maybe even ruining, your friendship. Some possible solutions: You could decide that you're both going to "go for him," but you agree ahead of time not to let it affect your friendship; You could both decide to forget about him rather than risk your friendship; You could flip a coin; You could decide to let the one with the strongest feelings have the first chance. Of course, he may already be interested in one of you, so he may do the deciding. Or, he may not be interested in either of you, so it may not be a problem at all.

Whatever happens, try to keep a sense of humor about it all. And, remember, at your age boyfriends come and go, but a girl you're friends with now may be someone you'll know your whole life. So, don't lose your friendship over a boy.

9. *Suppose you've been good friends with a boy, but you want to be more than just friends with him?*

Friendships that turn into romances are extra special, so our advice would be: Go for it! However, remember that there's always the chance that your romantic feelings may get in the way of your friendship. So, it's best to think it over carefully and to take it slowly.

Before you tell him how you feel, try to be sure about your own feelings. Are you confusing friendship feelings with romantic feelings? Are your feelings likely to last or might they change again sometime soon? Unless, or until, you're pretty sure of your feelings, it's probably better to hold off telling him about your feelings.

You also need to think about what might happen if he doesn't feel the same way toward you. Will one or both of you start feeling awkward or weird around each other? Perhaps it would be best to bring the topic up in a more roundabout way, rather than simply coming right out with it. Instead of telling him how you feel, you might ask him something like, "Does it ever bother you that people sometimes think we're boyfriend and girlfriend instead of just friends?" or "Have you ever wondered what it would be like if we ever started dating?" Chances are that he'll guess what is behind such questions. His answer may tell you that he doesn't feel the same way. But, since you haven't actually come right out and said how you feel, he can act as if he hasn't really understood what's behind the questions and you can do the same. This little bit of pretending may save a lot of embarrassment and keep you from feeling weird or awkward later on.

You should also give some thought to how it might affect your friendship if you two do get together, only to break up later on. Perhaps one or both of you would find it difficult to go back to being just friends. Is having him as a boyfriend worth the chance that you might wind up losing his friendship?

If the two of you do get together, make sure that you spend some time talking about this whole issue and about how you can stay friends if you break up later on.

10. *What should you do if you like a boy, but none of your friends likes him and they're always putting him down?*

As a general rule, we'd say that you shouldn't pay too much attention to what your friends think. It's what *you* think that really counts. The only exception to this rule would be when your friends actually have some pretty good reasons for not liking him. Some examples of good reasons might be the fact that he's a bully, that he does mean or cruel things to other people, that he takes drugs, that he drinks, or even drives a car when he's been drinking. Things like this don't necessarily mean he's a bad person, but he may be bad for you to have as a boyfriend.

In many cases, though, your friends' reasons for not liking him may not be very good ones. They may not like his "looks," the way he combs his hair, or the clothes he wears. Or, perhaps they don't like him because he isn't very "cool," isn't very popular, or isn't part of the in-crowd. Or, it may be that your friends are down on him because of an opinion they formed of him way back in grade school and they've never really given him a chance or taken the time to get to know him for who he is now.

It may be awfully hard to go against your friends, but if their reasons for not liking him aren't very good ones, don't let their opinions get to you! Try to get them to see his good points by explaining why you like him. If they keep on criticizing him and this bothers you, tell them how you feel and ask them to stop. If they're really your friends, they will. If they won't stop, perhaps you should think about finding new friends. Above all, don't let their criticisms "poison" your feelings for him.

11. *What if you like two boys and you can't decide which one you like best? Is it okay to have more than one boyfriend at a time?*

There's just no reason why a girl shouldn't feel free to date as many people as she wants, or to like two, three, ten, twenty, or however many boys as she wants.

If you like two boys and can't decide which one you like best, then why decide? Why not go right on liking both of them without worrying about choosing between them? If you have more than one boyfriend or want to date more than just one person, then why not go right ahead and have as many boyfriends and dates as you have the time for? As long as you're honest and you don't go around pretending to any of these boys that he's "the only one," then we say you should feel perfectly free to do whatever pleases you.

In fact, we think it's a good idea not to get tied down to just one boy when you're young. You'll have plenty of time to choose someone to settle down with later on. You may even find that you'll do a better job of choosing a marriage partner later on if you've had a chance to date and to get to know lots of different boys while you're young.

But, we wouldn't want to kid you, liking more than one boy, having more than one boyfriend, or dating more than one person at a time may cause problems. One or more of these boys may lose interest in you if he feels that he's "just one of the crowd." Or, he may put pressure on you to choose between him and another boy. If you don't, he may decide to find a girl who will have him as her "one and only." Other people may give you a hard time as well. Some may be jealous. Some may think it's just not right for a girl to like more than one boy at once. Others may not understand or believe that you're being honest with these boys. You may be accused of being fickle, of stringing boys along, or of being a two-timer. If any of these things do happen, try not to let it get to you. After all, if you're being straightforward and honest and you feel good about what you're doing, that's what really counts!

12. *Suppose you want to date or have a boyfriend but your parents say, "no way"?*

Girls usually choose to handle this problem in one of three ways: 1) Sneak around behind their parents' backs; 2) Go along with their parents' rules and wait until their parents say they're old enough; 3) Try and change their parents' minds. Let's look at each of these three choices.

Sneaking around behind your parents' backs just isn't a good choice. Sooner or later, girls who do this almost always get caught. If you do get caught, you may get into a lot of trouble and may do serious damage to your relationship with your parents. In fact, your parents may find it hard to trust you in the future. Even if you don't get caught, you'll probably feel awfully guilty about lying and sneaking. Things like dating and having a boyfriend should be a fun and pleasurable part of our lives. Having to sneak around and lie makes it all a lot less fun. Besides, dating and having a boyfriend can sometimes complicate our lives. Who needs the added complication of having to go behind your parents' backs? In short, sneaking around behind your parents' backs just isn't worth the "price" you may have to pay.

On the other hand, it can be awfully hard to go along with your parents' rules and wait until you're older, especially if there's a special someone you'd like to date or have as a boyfriend. But, parents who make these sorts of rules aren't usually trying to be mean or unfair. They often have your best interests in mind and are trying to protect you from "getting in over your head" by starting your romantic life at too young an age. After all, life is long. You have a lot of years ahead of you. So, if your parents want you to wait, think honestly about it. Maybe they're right. If your parents say "no way," ask yourself these questions: Are the other kids my age allowed to date and have boyfriends? Would I really lose anything by waiting until I'm older?

If your honest answer to these two questions is no, then perhaps waiting is the best choice for you. If, however, you feel that your parents are being too strict or too old-fashioned, you might want to consider the third choice.

Changing your parents' minds probably wouldn't be an easy job, but, it's worth a try. For starters, find out exactly why they've made these rules. What are they worried about? Once you understand their feelings, you may be able to come up with a compromise. If, for instance, your parents think you're "too young" to go out with a boy, maybe they'd allow you to go on group dates. Or, if they won't allow dates for the movies, perhaps they'll allow you to go to a boy-girl party or invite a boy to your house.

When you're talking this over with your parents, make use of the communication skills you learned in Part Two of this book. Use I-messages instead of you-messages. If necessary, arrange a problem-solving session.

13. *How do you know if you're really in love?*

Emotions can't be weighed or measured and different people have different ideas of what it means to be in love. So, we can't give you a definite answer to this question. But, we can share with you some of our thoughts on the subject.

We think it's important to recognize the differences between infatuation and true love. Infatuation is an intense, exciting (and sometimes confusing or scary) fireworks kind of feeling. We may be so wrapped up in our infatuation that it's hard to think about anything else or even to eat. People sometimes mistake infatuation for love. But, infatuation doesn't usually last very long; true love does. You may start out being infatuated and have it grow into true love. Or, the infatuation may pass and you may discover that this person really wasn't right for you after all. Also, you don't have to know someone very well in order to be infatuated. But, in order to truly love someone, you have to know that person (both their good points and bad points) very well. Moreover, infatuation can happen all of the sudden: true love takes more time.

Regardless of whether your relationship starts with a fireworks, infatuation kind of feeling or develops more slowly and gradually, sooner or later love relationships go through a questioning stage, where one or both of you begin to question whether this relationship is really a good one. During this questioning stage, one or the other of you may decide to end the relationship. In our opinion, it's only after you go through this questioning stage and decide to stay together, that you're really on the road to true love.

During the questioning stage, you might want to ask yourself these questions: Am I tired or unhappy most of the time? Does the relationship seem like more of a problem than a joy? Do I keep hoping that "maybe things will get better?" Do either of us frequently ask, "Do you really love me?" Do we find it impossible to spend a day together without having a fight? Do I often have to be careful about expressing certain opinions for fear that he might get mad at me? If you answer yes to one or more of these questions, then, chances are that you're not really in love after all, and that it's time to make a change in your relationship.

14. *How can you break up with your boyfriend without hurting his feelings?*

Sometimes, it's just not possible to avoid hurting someone's feelings, even if you don't want to. But, it's better for both of you to end the relationship rather than pretending that you still feel the way you did before.

It's best to tell him yourself, rather than having a friend do it or having him hear it through the grapevine. If he hears it from someone else, he's going to feel even worse. He may feel like you've made a fool of him in front of his friends, or that you didn't even care enough about him to bother being honest with him. He's probably going to feel hurt and angry with you for ending the relationship, but he'll feel even more hurt and even angrier if he hears the bad news from someone else.

It's usually very difficult for us to be honest and to tell someone that our feelings have changed. Even though it's perfectly normal and natural for a person's feelings to change, we may, nonetheless, feel awfully guilty about it. We may feel that we're some terrible, disloyal, bad sort of person. Sometimes, we may feel so guilty, so disloyal, and so afraid of his angry, hurt feelings that we do things like picking a fight with him so we'll have an "excuse" for breaking up with him. Rather than honestly admitting the real reason we want to end the relationship, we may try to shift the "blame" to him. We may try to pretend that it's his fault, that it's something he's done or something about him as a person that's causing the breakup. But, if you think about it, is it really right or really fair to shift the "blame?"

Our advice is: Be honest, but be kind. You might say something like, "I really want to be your friend, but I don't want to be tied down to just one person." Or "You're really terrific and I really care about you, but my feelings are changing and I just feel that I'm too young to settle down or to date only one person."

Finding Answers to
Your Other Questions

As we explained at the beginning of the last section, we've been asked hundreds and hundreds of questions over the years by the kids in our classes, by readers who've written to us, and by the people we've interviewed. There simply wasn't room in this book to cover all these questions. The list on pages 59–60 is far from complete. In fact, there are whole categories or classes of very commonly asked questions that we didn't mention at all. For instance, even though girls frequently ask questions about things like kissing, necking, petting, having sex, sexual decision-making, and morals, we didn't include any of these sorts of questions on the list. There are also other topics—jealousy, going steady, and reputations (to mention just a few)—that simply weren't covered on the list. So, if you have questions that weren't on the list or weren't covered anywhere else in this book, please don't think your questions are odd or unusual or that no one else has questions like yours. It's just that we simply didn't have enough space to get around to everything.

If you have questions that haven't been answered in this book, you might try looking through the list of books on pages 142–144. Perhaps one of these books will have the answers you're looking for.

Or, you might try asking someone you know, your mom, your dad, another relative, a teacher, or another adult you know. In some cases, asking someone your own age might be helpful, although sometimes friends our own age don't really know much more than we do.

The person you ask may or may not have answers that are helpful to you. But, sometimes it helps simply to have the chance to ask, to bring the topic up, and to talk it over with another person.

In the future, we plan to write another book that will answer at least some of these questions that we didn't have room for in this book. You could help make our next book better by sharing your questions with us. If you have a question that you've had trouble answering or one that you think we ought to include in our next book, please write and tell us about it. If you'd like us to write back, include a self-addressed, stamped envelope along with your letter. Send your letters to:

Lynda and Area Madaras
c/o Newmarket Press
18 East 48th Street
New York, New York 10017

2/ YOUR PARENTS

1: INTRODUCTION

In this part of the book, we'll be talking about your relationship with your parents. But, before we get started, we want to clear up one thing.

We'll be using the words "parent," "parents," "mother," and "father" a lot in this section. At times, the way we use these words may make it sound as if we're automatically assuming that all kids live in families where there are two, natural or "birth" parents living in the same house. But, as you know, this isn't always true. Because of death, divorce, or for some other reason, there are many kids who don't live with both their birth parents. For instance, some kids live in single parent families headed by a mother or father or live mainly with one parent, but visit or live part-time with the other parent. Some kids live with foster or stepparents, with grandparents, or other relatives or with friends of the family. Some kids live with dad and his girlfriend or mom and her boyfriend. You name it—there are all kinds of family living situations! So, if the words "parent," "parents," "mother," or "father" don't quite apply to the adult or adults you live with, just substitute words that do. The information, ideas, and suggestions in this chapter will work for you no matter what kind of family living situation you have.

FREEWRITING EXERCISE

Since this book is about you, let's start by asking you to explain your family living situation. Do you live with: one parent; two parents; mom; dad; step or foster parents; grandparents; other relatives; family friend? Use the blank space below to freewrite about the adult or adults you live with.

Gripes and Complaints

In order to write this section of the book, we talked to lots of preteens and teens and asked them to tell us about the kinds of fights, conflicts, and problems they had in getting along with their parents and why they thought they were having these problems.

In answer to our questions, we heard about ten jillion gripes and complaints. Some of the gripes we heard seemed ... well, they seemed a little unreasonable or even silly. For instance, one thirteen-year-old girl who was planning a party complained:

> *All my friends' parents let them drink beer and smoke pot. Everyone will expect to do it at my party. My mother is just so old-fashioned about some stuff. . . . I really love my parents though and I know that if I ever got into trouble or something, they'd be there for me. I can count on them.*

However, a number of kids said that their relationship with their parents wasn't so great. In fact, many kids said that they had a lot of fights, conflicts, and problems in getting along with their parents. Actually, it didn't come as a big surprise to find that many of the teens and preteens and parents we talked to were having problems in their relationships with each other. The growing-up years can sometimes be pretty hard on the way parents and kids get along. In fact, these years are sometimes called "the stormy years" because parents and kids so often run into fights and conflicts with each other during these years.

THE STORMY YEARS

When we asked the kids we interviewed about this storminess, about the problems with their parents and about why they had these problems, we got many different answers. For instance, some kids said that they had problems with their parents over things like curfews, dress codes, rules, and regulations. Other kids said that their parents treated them like babies. Still other kids said that their parents put too much pressure on them to be some kind of a superstar or that their parents were disappointed in them because they weren't living up to their parents' expectations. Some kids said they just couldn't talk to their parents. Other kids felt that their parents were too busy to even have any time for them. Some even felt that their parents didn't really love them.

As we say, we got many different answers, far too many to cover them all in this one book! But, certain kinds of problems come up over and over again, and we'd like to mention a few of them.

"The stormy years" The preteen and teen years are sometimes called this because parents and kids so often run into fights, conflicts, and problems during these years.

FIGHTS OVER RULES AND REGULATIONS

Some kids said they had problems getting along with their parents because their parents were "too strict" or "too old-fashioned." Others said that their parents tried to run their lives or treated them like they were still little kids. Here's what two of them had to say:

> *My life is run by my parents. They tell me when to get up, when to go to bed, when to do my homework, what to eat. They don't let me run my own life. They act like I'm about two years old.*
>
> —Ginny, age 11

> *They're so strict. I'm not allowed to date or have boyfriends or do any-thing that my friends are allowed to do . . . My parents don't trust me . . . They can't realize the fact that I'm old enough to make decisions on my own.*
>
> —Casey, age 15

When you think about it, it's not too surprising that kids and parents have hassles over things like curfews, rules and regulations, whether the kid is old enough to do certain things and what the kid is (and isn't) allowed to do. A parent's job is to make sure that their kids learn the things they will need to know in order to some day go out and make their own way in the world. The parent also has to make sure that the kid is protected and kept healthy and safe from harm until the kid is old enough to make safe and wise decisions for itself. If parents let kids do things on their own before the kids are ready, the kids could get into trouble. For instance, if a parent let a three-year-old cross the street before the kid knew enough to look both ways, the kid could get run over. So, parents hold the kid's hand until they're sure the kid is old enough to cross safely.

On the other hand, kids are usually in a big hurry to grow up and have more of a say in running their lives. They often think they're old enough to cross the street, to go out on dates, to stay out until after midnight, or to have more freedom and independence than their parents think they're ready for. In a way, it's kind of a tug of war between the kids wanting to make their own decisions and parents wanting them to wait until the parents are sure the kids are ready.

This tug of war can really heat up during the preteen and teen years. If you find that you and your parents are hassling over rules and regulations, curfews, dress codes, and so on, sections 2, 3, and 4 will help you learn some communication skills and ways of solving problems that will help ease this tug of war.

"I CAN'T TALK TO MY PARENTS"

Some kids had problems in their relationship with their parents because they couldn't really talk to their parents, as this girl explains:

> *I can't really talk to my parents, not about important things.*

> —Ellen, age 13

Some kids felt nervous or awkward about talking to their parents, like this eleven-year-old who said:

> *I get nervous when I try and talk to them. I can't really think of anything to say. I know they want me to be all friendly and tell them things, but I never know what to say.*

Some kids had trouble talking over sensitive subjects like sex with their parents, as this girl explained:

> *I can't talk to my parents about sex. If I even ask them a question, they act like I'm planning to go right out and have sex.*

Other kids complained that they couldn't talk with their parents without getting into a fight; as this girl put it:

> *I don't know why it is, my mom and I say about two words to each other . . . bam. We wind up fighting. I guess we just push each other's buttons. I'd rather skip talking to her than have these giant fights constantly.*

If you have trouble talking to your parents about a specific topic, such as sex, you may need to bring up the topic yourself or to suggest that you and your parents read some helpful books together. Or, if you generally feel nervous and never quite know what to say to your parents, it helps to remember that you really do have the words you need inside your head. (If you can just put what you're feeling into words, you'll be able to communicate!) You may also want to pay particular attention to Section 2, which will help you learn some new communication skills.

Or if, like Liza, you can't seem to talk to your parents without getting into a fight, it might be helpful to learn some new ways of communicating. Sections 2, 3, and 4 will show you how the way you talk and the way you listen can help you to avoid fights and to start solving your problems.

PRESSURES AND EXPECTATIONS

Some kids said that they had problems with their parents because their parents expected too much of them or put too much pressure on them. Here's what some of these kids had to say:

> *My parents expect me to be some kind of superstar. No matter how well I do, they want me to do better. . . . Like if I got a 95, they want to know why I didn't get a hundred.*
>
> —Janice, age 12

> *My mom expects me to be as popular as she was. She's always bugging me about why I don't have more friends over or go to parties or have dates. . . . I'm just not this great popular kid.*
>
> —Betsy, age 15

> *My older sister was like this perfect person. She got straight A's and was the class president. My parents and teachers are always saying, "Your sister Caroline this; your sister Caroline that." They're always comparing me to her.*
>
> —Patsy, age 14

> *My parents think I'm a failure because I'm not like them. They think I'm their opportunity to make themselves over again . . . I can never do enough to please them.*
>
> —Alice, age 12

Kids whose parents put too much pressure on them or expect them to live up to some certain standard often feel deeply resentful and angry. Or, they may feel as if they're a disappointment to their parents. They may even get to feeling that there's something wrong with them because they don't measure up to their parents' expectations and standards.

If your parents put too much pressure on you or are making you unhappy with their expectations, you need to let your parents know how you feel. Communicating these kinds of feelings can be difficult. The next section will teach you some ways of communicating that can help you let your parents know how you feel. Oftentimes, parents don't even realize that you feel upset by their pressure or expectations. Many times, parents will change once they realize how you're feeling.

But, we wouldn't want to kid you. Sometimes, no matter how well you express your feelings, your parents will continue pressuring you. If this is the case, it's important for you to remember that you're fine just the way you are, even if you don't meet your parents' expectations. If you start feeling bad about yourself, it might be helpful for you to talk over your feelings with someone else. The section "Getting Help" at the back of this book will give you suggestions on how to find someone to talk to.

FEELING UNLOVED

Some kids said that they don't think their parents really loved or cared about them. Here's what some kids had to say.

> *My parents never have any time for me. They're always too busy. I don't think they really care about me.*
>
> —John, age 11

> *I don't think my mom really loves me. She wouldn't act like she does toward me if she loved me.*
>
> —Sara, age 12

> *My dad never shows me any affection.*
>
> —Penelope, age 10

> *My parents let me do whatever I want. . . . They don't care enough to bother to make rules. Half the time they don't even know where I am or what I'm doing. They could care less.*
>
> —June, age 15

If like Penelope, your parents don't show affection, it's easy to get the feeling that your parents don't really love you. Or, if like John, your parents are always too busy to spend time with you, it's easy to start thinking that they don't really care. But, if you'd like more affection from your parents or more of their time, it's important for you to let your parents know how you're feeling. Sometimes, parents love their kids very much but they have a hard time showing affection, or they forget to take time out of their busy lives. If you can let them know how you're feeling, there's at least a chance, and maybe a good chance, that they'll change. But, you first need to let them know how you're feeling. Section 2 will help you learn how to communicate in such a way that your parents will really understand how you're feeling.

But, here again, we don't want to kid you. It's sad to say, but it's true: There are some parents who just aren't very loving and just don't seem to care. We wish this weren't true, but it is. It can be very, very painful for you if your parents don't care. You can do your best to let them know how you feel, how much you're hurting and how much you want them to care. But, nothing you do can change things unless they're ready and willing to change. If you feel that your parents don't really love you, you might start to get the feeling that you're not loveable. If so, please remember that even though your parents don't care, you're still a special, worthwhile person. It might be helpful for you to find someone to talk to about your parents and about your feelings. For some suggestions as to who you might talk to, see the section "Getting Help," at the end of the book.

OTHER SERIOUS PROBLEMS

We're sorry to say that some of the kids we talked to had very serious problems in their relationships with their parents. We talked to kids who were victims of physical or sexual abuse. We talked to families where the parents, or the kids themselves, had drug or alcohol problems. We talked to kids who had such serious problems in their relationship with their parents (or in some other area of their life) that they had run away from home or had even considered suicide.

If you have these very serious sorts of problems, the communication skills in the next few sections aren't going to be much help. You may even need more help than this book (or any book for that matter) can give you. We hope you'll get that help. The section "Getting Help" (in Part Three) will tell you how to go about getting the help you need.

2: SENDING THE MESSAGE

     In this and the next two sections we'll be teaching you some communication skills that can help you improve your relationship with your parents. As we will explain, communication has two parts: 1) sending the message, or talking, and 2) receiving the message, or listening. In this section, we'll be concentrating on the first part of communication, sending the message. We'll be showing you some new ways of talking to your parents that will help you avoid fights and conflicts and will get you started on the road to solving your problems.

    But, before you begin, we want to remind you to do the quizzes and exercises in this section and the next two (3 and 4) *in order.* In other parts of this book, you can feel free to skip around and do things out of order, according to whatever interests you most at the particular time, but in these three sections you really shouldn't skip around. The quizzes and exercises in these sections should be done in order. You should start with Exercise #1 in this section and work straight through to the end of Section 4 without skipping around. Of course, you don't have to do these chapters in one sitting. Take your time. But the exercises and quizzes in these chapters build on information you've learned by doing the previous quizzes and exercises. Some of the later quizzes and exercises just won't make sense unless you've already done the earlier ones.

    To get started, try Exercise #1.

Communication has two parts.

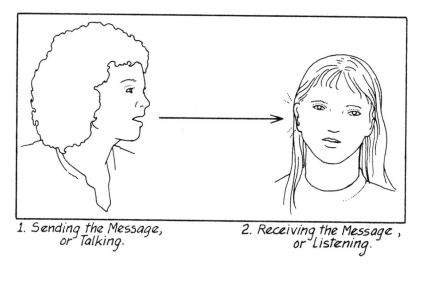

1. Sending the Message,
   or Talking.

2. Receiving the Message,
   or Listening.

EXERCISE #1

After each of the situations below, you will find two responses. Read each situation and both of the possible responses, and then, put an X in front of the response you'd most like your parent to make if *you* were in that situation. Take your time and choose carefully. Remember, you are not choosing the response your parent would probably make; you're picking the response you'd most *like* your parent to make. (You may not be real crazy about either response, but pick one.)

Situation One: Your room is a total mess—a regular disaster area. Your mom goes into your room to put clean sheets on your bed, but there's so much junk on the floor, she can't get through the door. She says:

☐ **1.** "Young lady, your room looks like a pig pen. How can you live like that? You're a complete slob!"

☐ **2.** "When I see your clothes and things spread all over the floor like that, I am furious. I feel like throwing the whole mess in the trash."

Situation Two: You were supposed to mow the lawn on Saturday afternoon. You didn't do it. Your dad says:

☐ **1.** "You are *so* lazy! I just can't depend on you to do anything around here, can I?"

□ **2.** "When the lawn isn't mowed, I get so mad I can hardly see straight. I count on the yard looking nice. It's really important to me."

Situation Three: You've just come home from school, all excited about the "A" you got on your math test. Your dad is in the kitchen making his famous spaghetti sauce for dinner. You come barging in the kitchen door, leaving the door open. Your dad says:

□ **1.** "What's the matter with you? You always leave the kitchen door wide open!"

□ **2.** "It bugs me when the kitchen door is left open like that. I don't want flies in the food!"

Situation Four: You decide to go to the mall after school to play video games. You're supposed to leave a note when you go somewhere, but you forgot. Your mom comes home from work. You're not home and there's no note. When you finally get home, your mom says:

□ **1.** "Where have you been? How many times have I told you to leave a note if you're going someplace? You just can't be counted on, can you?"

□ **2.** "When I got home and you weren't here and there wasn't a note, I was worried sick. I didn't know if you were safe or if something terrible had happened."

Situation Five: Your dad is trying to explain something to you. You're not really very interested in what he's saying, and besides, you've got something you want to say. Instead of waiting for him to finish, you butt right in and say what you want to say. Your dad says:

□ **1.** "How come you keep interrupting me? Where did you learn your manners?"

□ **2.** "I find it very difficult to speak when I can't complete a single sentence."

Situation Six: Your family is sitting down to dinner, and the dog is begging because you forgot to feed him. Your mom says:

□ **1.** "You are so inconsiderate! Your dog is starving because you couldn't be bothered to take a few minutes to feed him."

□ **2.** "I get so mad when the dog is begging at the table because he hasn't been fed. It makes me want to scream and yell!"

Situation Seven: Your mom lends you her necklace and you lose it at school. Your mom says:

□ **1.** "You did what? You lost my jewelry! How could you be so incredibly irresponsible?"

☐ **2.** "I get really aggravated when I lend something and it isn't taken care of. That necklace was really special to me and now it's gone."

Situation Eight: Your allowance is supposed to cover all your "extras." But, you've already spent your allowance. You need five dollars for a field trip that your class is taking tomorrow. You ask your dad for the money. He says:

☐ **1.** "You act like money just grows on trees! You never think ahead and plan your expenses. You just spend and spend and expect me to pay for everything. You just don't know the value of money, do you?"

☐ **2.** "I get really upset when I'm asked for money at the last minute. It feels like I'm being taken advantage of. I'm upset when I'm asked for money above and beyond allowances, because I only have so much to give."

Situation Nine: You're watching your favorite TV show with the volume turned up full blast. Your dad comes into the room and says:

☐ **1.** "How many times do I have to tell you to turn that thing down! You never listen, do you? You are so inconsiderate! You never think about anyone but yourself!

☐ **2.** "Turn that thing down. It's so loud I can't hear myself think. It's really a drag to have to come in here and ask to have the TV turned down!

Situation Ten: You're doing the dishes after dinner. You drop and break your mom's favorite crystal serving bowl. Your mom hears the crash and comes into the kitchen. She looks at the broken bowl, which is in a million pieces on the floor, and says:

☐ **1.** "How could you be so clumsy? You are always so careless! I just can't trust you to do anything right, can I?"

☐ **2.** "Carelessness like this really gets to me! That was my favorite bowl. I'm just heartbroken to see it ruined."

SCORING EXERCISE #1

If you're like most people, you probably checked box #2 for most or all of these situations. If you checked box #1 for most or all of these situations, read the material in the following pages and try this exercise again. If you need to do the exercise again, be sure that you check the box that indicates the response you'd *most like to hear* in that situation, not the response you'd probably really get from your parents.

You-Messages and I-Messages

There's a reason why people like to hear the kind of responses that appear after Box #2, instead of the responses that appear after Box #1. The responses that appear after Box #1 are what the famous psychologist Dr. Thomas Gordon calls you-messages. The responses that appear after Box #2 are what Dr. Gordon calls I-messages.

As Dr. Gordon and others have pointed out, there's a *big* difference between you-messages and I-messages. You-messages usually make the person hearing the message feel angry, hurt, defensive, uptight, or just plain lousy. You-messages put the other person down. They blame and accuse the other person. They attack the other person's whole personality, rather than attacking just the problem or situation at hand. You-messages tend to block communication and start fights.

I-messages let the other person know how you're feeling, but they are much less likely to make the other person feel attacked, put-down, or angry. I-messages don't talk about what *always* or what *never* happens. Rather, I-messages talk about the specific situation or the problem that's going on right at that particular moment. They don't attack the other person's whole personality or say bad things about what the other person is like as a human being. I-messages tend to *open* communication, and are much less likely to start fights.

HOW YOU-MESSAGES WORK

Let's look a little more closely at exactly how you-messages work.

You-messages accuse the other person:

"*You* did this; *you* did that."

"*You* didn't do this; *you* didn't do that."

Or, you-messages find fault with the other person:

"*You're* to blame. It's *your* fault."

Or, you-messages put the other person down:

"*You're* a slob. *You're* irresponsible. *You're* unfair. *You're* stupid. *You're* ... whatever."

You-messages start fights because when people feel blamed, accused, or put down, they feel like they're being attacked. And when people feel like they're being attacked, they are apt to get *defensive*. They defend themselves from the attack. People have lots of different ways of defending themselves from attack, but two of the most common responses we have when we're attacked are to deny or to fight back.

So, when someone sends a you-message like: "It's your fault!" or "You're to blame!" or "You can't be trusted," the other person usually starts to argue back by denying the you-message: "It's not my fault!" or "I'm not to blame!" or "I can *too* be trusted." Or, they may counterattack with a you-message of their own: "It's not my fault, it's *your* fault!"—"I'm not to blame, *you* are!"—"I can be trusted, it's *you* who can't be trusted!" And before you know it, you've got a full-scale

You-messages block communication and start fights.

When one person sends a You-Message that attacks, blames, accuses, or puts the other person down, the other person defends himself or herself by:

Denying the You-Message and/or Counterattacking with another You-Message:

Then the You-Messages start flying back and forth

and communication breaks down completely.

fight going on. The you-messages start flying back and forth. Things get hot and heavy, and pretty soon, communication has broken down altogether. For example, take a look at this you-message fight between a parent and teenage daughter.

Parent: Young lady, where have you been? You were supposed to be home at ten o'clock and it's past midnight. You just can't be trusted, can you? *(Parent attacks with a you-message.)*

Daughter: Oh great! I walk in the door and you just automatically jump down my throat. You don't even give me a chance to explain. *(Daughter counterattacks with a you-message of her own, accusing her parents of not giving her a chance to explain.)*

Parent: I've listened to far too many of your excuses. I've had it up to here with you and your excuses! You just don't care about anyone but yourself, do you? *(Parent denies the daughter's you-message and comes back with one.)*

Daughter: You're the one who doesn't care. I could have been dead or something and all you care about is yelling at me. You never listen to my side of the story. *(Daughter denies parent's you-message and adds fuel to the fire with yet another you-message.)*

Parent: Don't you talk to me in that tone of voice, young lady! I've put up with about all I'm going to take from you. You're grounded! No parties, no dates, no football games, no nothing for the rest of the month! *(Communication breaks down completely.)*

This fight might have been avoided if the parent and daughter had used I-messages instead of you-messages. In a few pages, we'll show you how I-messages could have helped avoid this fight, but before we do that, we'd like you to think for a moment about you-message fights you may have had with your parents.

EXERCISE #2

Does the fight between this parent and daughter sound at all familiar to you? Have you and your parents ever gotten yourselves backed into a corner with you-messages? Use the space below to describe a you-message fight you've had with your parents. If you can't think of one right off the bat, keep your ears open; we bet you'll come across one sooner or later. When you do, describe the situation briefly here. Then answer the questions.

_____

_____

_____

_____

_____

1. What you-messages did your parent use? (If you can't remember the exact words, just come as close as you can.)_____

_____

_____

_____

2. What you-messages did you use?_____

_____

_____

_____

3. How did your parent's you-messages make you feel?_____

_____

_____

_____

4. How did you respond to your parent's you-messages? Did you use you-messages in responding to your parents? If so, write the you-messages here: ____

_____

_____

_____

5. How did your parents react to any you-messages that you may have used? Did they respond by using more you-messages, by getting madder, by sending you to your room? What happened?

_____

_____

_____

6. How did things turn out? Were you happy with the way things turned out? Why or why not?_____

_____

_____

_____

EXERCISE #3

Below is a list of the kind of you-messages that parents often send to their children and a list of you-messages that kids often send their parents. Have you ever heard or used these you-messages or similar ones? Put a check mark next to those that sound like something you or your parents have said. Then use the blank spaces to add other you-messages that you or your parents have used.

1. YOU-MESSAGES PARENTS USE:

☐ Why don't you ever listen?

☐ Why don't you grow up?

☐ You only think of yourself.

☐ You just don't know when to stop, do you?

☐ Can't you act your age?

☐ You think the world owes you a living, don't you?

☐ Don't you know any better?

☐ You just won't listen, will you?

☐ You can't be trusted.

☐ You don't have any respect.

☐ You are *so* lazy!

☐ _____

☐ _____

☐ _____

☐ _____

☐ _____

☐ _____

☐ _____

2. YOU-MESSAGES KIDS USE:

☐ You don't believe in me.

☐ You don't understand me.

☐ You never take my side.

☐ You're not being fair.

☐ You never give me a chance.

☐ Everything always has to be your way.

☐ You always treat me like a baby.

☐ You don't want me to have any fun.

☐ You're so old-fashioned.

☐ You never let me do anything I want to do.

☐ You always want to be the boss.

☐ _____

☐ _____

☐ _____

☐ _____

☐ _____

☐ _____

☐ _____

EXERCISE #4

Now, read back over your answers to Exercise #2 and #3 and then answer these two questions.

1. How true, accurate, or correct are the you-messages you send your parents? For example, if you've used a you-message like "You treat me like a baby," is this true? Do your parents treat you like a baby?

Look over Exercise #2 and the list in Exercise #3, and decide how much truth there is in your you-messages? A lot? Some? A little? None at all?

_____

_____

2. How well do you-messages work for you? When you've used you-messages with your parents, how have things turned out? Are you happy with what happens when you use you-messages?

_____

_____

_____

_____

_____

_____

_____

_____

COMMENTS ON EXERCISE #4

If you're like most kids, there's probably some truth—and maybe *a lot* of truth—to your you-messages. But, your you-messages probably aren't 100% correct, simply because very few parents act the exact same way *all* the time. However, even if your you-messages aren't 100 percent true or accurate, it's unlikely that they are *totally* untrue or *totally* inaccurate. There's probably *some* truth to them. For instance, your parents may well treat you like a baby sometimes or even most of the time. Or, it may be perfectly true that your parents don't let you do very many (and practically any!) of the things you'd like to do.

No doubt about it. Truth and justice are on your side! You're right and they're wrong! (At least some of the time.)

But, this isn't always what's important. As many famous psychologists and authors like Alex Packer, Adele Faber, and Elaine Mazlish have pointed out, sometimes *it doesn't really matter* whether or not your you-messages are 100 percent true. What matters is, do they do the job for you?

Your answer to this question will depend on just what you want your you-messages to do. If you want to blow off steam, you-messages work very well. And, when we're feeling really angry or hurt or frustrated, we may well *need* to blow off some steam, and sometimes it's healthy for us to do so.

But many times you may want to do more than simply have a chance to yell about your "rightness" and your parents "wrongness." You may want your parents to hear what you are saying and to take your complaints seriously. You may even be hoping to change the situation or behavior that's causing you problems. You-messages can sometimes work in changing a situation or behavior, but as a rule, I-messages work better than you-messages.

As we explained, you-messages tend to make the listener uptight and to start fights. I-messages tend to do just the opposite. Of course, using I-messages doesn't automatically mean that your parents will come around to seeing things your way. But I-messages have a better shot at working than you-messages do.

In the next few pages we'll be teaching you more about I-messages and how to put them to work for you.

I-Messages

Reread the responses that appear after the second boxes in Exercise #1 (on pages 82–84). These kinds of responses are called I-messages.

I-messages often work better than you-messages because they avoid placing blame, accusing the other person, insulting the other person, or putting the other person down. Therefore, they are less likely to make the other person uptight or defensive. I-messages are less likely to invite denial and counterattacks. I-messages talk about just *one* situation, not what *always* or *never* happens. They can open, rather than block, communication. You're *more* likely to have things go your way if you use an I-message rather than a you-message.

Remember the teenage daughter and parent who got into a you-message fight a few pages ago? Let's see what might have happened if the parent had used I-messages instead of you-messages.

Parent: When it got past 10 o'clock and I didn't know where you were, I began to get worried. I've been worried sick for the last two hours!

Daughter: I'm sorry you were so worried. Susan's car broke down. We walked to the gas station and got someone to help us. I tried to call, but the phone was out of order. I'm really sorry.

Parent: Well, I'm glad to hear that you tried to call. And the important thing is that you're home safe and sound!

Look what happened this time. Instead of greeting the daughter at the door with a bunch of you-messages, the parent used an I-message to tell the daughter how worried the parent had been. Because she didn't feel blamed or attacked, the daughter didn't feel the need to deny or counterattack with you-messages of her own. The I-message opened up, rather than blocked, communication. The daughter had a chance to tell her side of the story. A fight was avoided.

What might have happened if the parent had used you-messages? Could the daughter have saved the day by using I-messages? Let's see.

Parent: Young lady, where have you been? You were supposed to be home at 10 o'clock, and it's past midnight. You just can't be trusted, can you? *(Parent is using you-messages again.)*

Daughter: Can I have a chance to explain? *(The daughter doesn't get hooked into the parent's you-message.)*

Parent: No, I've listened to far too many of your excuses. I've had it up to here with you and your excuses! I don't need to hear anymore excuses. You just don't care about anyone but yourself, do you? *(The parent continues sending you-messages.)*

Daughter: I wish I could have a moment to explain. *(The daughter still maintains her cool. She doesn't add fuel to the fight by sending you-messages.)*

Parent: I don't know if I want to listen to you. *(The parent is still mad, but is losing steam. Without the added fuel of counterattacking you-messages, the fight is beginning to burn itself out).*

Daughter: When I have a good explanation and don't have a chance to say anything, I feel so frustrated that I don't really know what I should do. *(Amazing! The daughter not only keeps her cool, but she even manages to send an I-message which cools things out even more.)*

Parent: Oh, all right, tell me your story.

Daughter: The car broke down. We walked to the gas station and got help, but it took a long time. I knew you'd be worried. I tried to call but the phone was broken. I really did try! I'm awfully sorry you were so upset.

Parent: Well, I guess you did all you could in the situation. I'm sorry I blew up at you like that. It's just that I was half out of my mind with worry.

Daughter: I *am* sorry.

Parent: Me too.

Once again, the I-messages saved the day! By avoiding you-messages and using an I-message, the daughter kept the communication open and avoided a fight.

Of course, this all sounds pretty good on paper. The truth of the matter is that things don't always go so smoothly in real life. We can't promise you that things will turn out this well for you. But, as we've said, you've got a better chance of having things go your way with I-messages than you do when you use blaming, accusing you-messages.

HOW TO SEND I-MESSAGES

Psychologists like Dr. Gordon and others have developed three steps that will help you send I-messages. I-messages don't always have to include all three steps, and they don't have to be done in this exact order. But, if you're just learning to use I-messages, it helps to follow these steps.

Step 1: First, describe the situation or behavior that is causing problems for you. Be specific, talk about one situation, not what *always* or *never* happens. Just describe the situation or behavior. Avoid name calling, accusing, and blaming. In fact, if at all possible, avoid using the word *you* altogether. For example:

> *"When I'm not allowed to use the telephone after 8:00 at night . . ."*

> *"When I can't have friends stay overnight on school nights . . ."*

Avoiding the use of the word *you* is important. The examples sound much better than "When you won't let me use the telephone after 8:00 at night . . ." and "When you won't let me have friends stay overnight on school nights . . ."

Step 2: Second, describe how you *feel* when this situation or behavior occurs. For example:

> *"When I'm not allowed to use the phone after 8:00 at night, I feel really upset."*

Step 1	Step 2	Step 3
Describe the situation, but avoid using the word "you."	Describe how you feel when this situation occurs.	Explain why you feel this way.

Sending I-messages.

"When I can't have friends stay overnight on school nights, I feel I'm being treated unfairly."

Step 3: Then, explain *why* you feel this way. For example:

"When I'm not allowed to use the phone after 8:00 at night, I feel really upset. Sometimes I need Susie to explain something about homework. Other times, I'd just like a chance to talk with Susie. I also feel upset because the other kids at school tease me about not being allowed to use the phone."

"When I can't have friends stay overnight on a school night, I feel that I'm being treated unfairly because my older sister was allowed to have friends stay overnight on school nights when she was my age."

Now, remember, sending I-messages instead of you-messages doesn't automatically mean that your parents will agree to let you talk on the phone after eight o'clock, have friends over on school nights, or whatever. But, using I-messages does increase the chances of your parents taking you seriously and being willing to talk things over. I-messages at least open up the possibility of communicating further. And, with some luck, things just might go your way! In any case, you're bound to do better with an I-message in these situations than with a you-message like "You always treat me like a baby!" or "You're not being fair!"

EXERCISE #5

Using I-messages instead of you-messages can make things a lot easier for you, but practice makes perfect. Try turning the you-messages in the following situations into I-messages. Read the situation. Then read the you-message response we've written for you. Next, think how you might turn the you-message into an I-message. Write your I-message in the blank space.

1. Your brother (who's only 1½ years older than you) gets $5.00 more allowance than you do. You decide to ask your parents to raise your allowance. They say no.

You-message: But, you're not being fair, you give Jimmy $5.00 more than you give me. Jimmy always gets more of everything than I do!

I-message: _____

_____

_____

_____

_____

2. You cleaned up the whole house without even being asked to do it. When mother gets home from work all she says is, "You forgot to sweep the front porch."

You-message: You just don't appreciate anything I do. No matter what I do, it's never enough. See if I ever do anything for you again.

I-message: _____

_____

_____

_____

_____

3. Your best friend has two free tickets to a Madonna concert and she wants you to go with her. Your parents say no. They think you are too young to go to a concert.

You-message: You act like I was still a little kid. You never let me do anything I want to do. You don't want me to have any fun.

I-message: _____

_____

_____

_____

_____

4. You just bought some make-up for the first time. You put on a little bit of light lipstick, a little bit of blush-on, a touch of mascara, and just a hint of blue eye-shadow. Your dad goes nuts when he sees you. He's acting like you look like a tramp. He tells you that you have to wash it off before you can leave the house.

You-message: You just don't want me to grow up. I'm not a baby anymore. You don't have any right to tell me what to do!

I-message: _____

_____

_____

_____

_____

5. You just brought home a terrific report card. All A's except for one C in French. The first thing your father says when he looks at your report card is, "How come you got a C in French?"

You-message: All you ever do is pick on me. You expect me to be some kind of superstar. You never give me credit for the good things I do. You didn't even see my A's. All you saw was the C.

I-message: _____

_____

_____

_____

6. Your little brother gets mad and hits you. You hit him back. He runs and tells your mother that you hit him. Your mother turns around and yells at you.

You-message: You always take his side. Anytime anything happens between him and me, you automatically think it's my fault.

I-message: _____

_____

_____

_____

7. Your mother has no respect for your privacy. She comes into your room without knocking. If you lock your door or even just close it, she wants to know what your doing in there.

You-message: You never give me a moment of privacy. You're so nosey.

I-message: _____

_____

_____

_____

8. You are on the telephone talking to your best friend. It doesn't seem to you that you've been on long at all, but your dad starts bugging you to get off. Finally, he's bugging you so much that you have to hang up.

You-message: You never let me talk to my friends. You talk for hours but I can't even use the phone for a few minutes without everyone bothering me.

I-message: _____

_____

_____

_____

9. All your friends are allowed to date. You're not. Now a guy in your English class has asked you to go to the movies. Your parents won't hear of it. They say you're much too young.

You-message: You are so old-fashioned. Everyone else's parents let them go out on dates. You never let me do anything. You act like I'm still about two years old.

I-message: _____

_____

_____

_____

10. You and your friends are going to the mall on Friday night. You tell your mom where you're going and when you'll be back, but that's not enough for her. She starts asking all kinds of questions about who you're going with, what you're going to do, exactly where you'll be. She's acting like you're some kind of criminal or something.

You-message: Can't you just leave me alone for a change? You never trust me. I've never done anything wrong and you act like I'm the worst person in the world.

I-message: _____

_____

_____

_____

ANSWERS FOR EXERCISE #5

Below is a list of sample answers for Exercise #5. Your answers needn't be just like ours. We just included them to give you an idea of some of the ways in which these you-messages can be changed into I-messages.

1. The fact that Jimmy gets more allowance feels unfair to me because, even though he's older, we both have the same kinds of expenses that we have to pay for out of our allowances.

2. When I've worked so hard cleaning the house and don't get thanked, I feel really hurt because it seems like the work I did wasn't appreciated.

3. Not being able to go to the concert makes me feel really down and disappointed because I'll be missing out on all that fun with my friends.

4. Not being able to wear make-up makes me feel totally out of it because the rest of my friends do.

5. When the one C I got gets more attention than all the A's, I feel awfully discouraged, as if the A's don't even count.

6. When I don't get a chance to tell my side, I feel hurt because it seems that his side of the story is more important than mine.

7. When my privacy isn't respected, I feel frustrated because I really feel a need for privacy now that I'm getting older.

8. When I have to get off the phone before I'm finished with my conversation, I feel really bugged because it's important to me to be able to talk with my friends.

9. I feel so disappointed about not going on this date because I really like this boy and I'd really enjoy getting to know him better.

10. When I'm asked for all these details, I feel angry because it feels like I'm not trusted.

EXERCISE #6

Remember back on page 87 when you described a you-message fight that you and your parents had? Now we're going to give you a chance to redo that fight. In the space below, retell the fight, only this time, have you and your parents use I-messages. Then answer these questions. Would using I-messages have worked better for you and/or for your parents? How might things have gone differently if you'd used I-messages instead of you-messages?

_____

_____

_____

_____

_____

_____

_____

_____

_____

_____

_____

EXERCISE #7

Now that you've had some practice on paper using I-messages, you can put them to work for you in real life. The next time a problem, fight, or conflict comes up, try using I-messages to deal with it.

Then, write a brief description of what happened and answer the questions below. _____

_____

_____

_____

_____

1. Were you able to use I-messages?_____

2. What I-messages did you use?_____

_____

_____

3. How did your parents react? What did they say?_____

_____

_____

_____

4. Did using I-messages help? If so, how?_____

_____

_____

_____

5. Did you have any problems using I-messages?_____

_____

_____

_____

6. Did either you or your parents use any you-messages? If so, what were they?

_____

_____

_____

WHAT TO DO WHEN I-MESSAGES DON'T WORK

If you've tried using I-messages and the whole thing fell flat on its face, don't give up! You and your parents have probably spent most of your lives using you-messages when you're having fights, problems, or conflicts. Using I-messages may be a totally new thing for you. Learning to do something new or different is always difficult. Remember when you were first learning to ride a two-wheeler bike? Did you just hop on the bike and go pedaling off into the sunset? No way. You fell off, skinned your knees, bumped your backside, and generally had some difficulties. Of course, learning to use I-messages isn't the same as learning to ride a bike. But, like learning any new skill, learning to communicate in new ways takes practice and patience, so hang in there.

If you had problems when you tried to use I-messages, you might ask yourself the following questions. Read through the following list and put a check mark in front of the items that may have been problems for you in Exercise #7 or may be in your future attempts at using I-messages.

☐ **1.** *Did I really use an I-message? Did I describe the problem-causing situation without name-calling, blaming, or accusing?*

It's easy to blow it by describing things in an accusing or blaming way without even realizing it. Consider, for example, the following message:

"When you act so old-fashioned and won't let me wear lipstick, I feel really out of it."

At first glance, this may sound like an I-message. But, if you look more closely, you'll see it's really a you-message. It puts the parent down by name-calling: "You're so old-fashioned." It blames the parent for the problem—"You won't let me wear lipstick." What it really says is, "You're to blame, you're at fault, you're causing the problem by being so old-fashioned and by not letting me wear lipstick."

Now, you may be perfectly right when you say your parents are old-fashioned and that their behavior (not letting you wear lipstick) is causing the problem. But, what's more important to you in a situation like this? Getting to say you're perfectly right, or getting to wear lipstick? If it's wearing lipstick you're after, you've got a better chance if you can send a real I-message.

Remember, one way of making sure you're really sending I-messages in situations like this is to avoid the word *you* altogether. For example, without the use of the word *you*, the above message might become, "When I can't wear lipstick, I feel really out of it."

Look back over your I-messages in Exercise #7. Did you use the word "you" in describing the situation or behavior that was causing you problems? Did you really use an I-message or did you describe the problem using name-calling, blaming, fault-finding or accusing?

☐ **2.** *Was my timing wrong?*

Timing has a lot to do with it. For instance, if you approach your parents with a wonderful I-message about getting a raise in your allowance, but you do it just before pay-day or when your parents just got their tax bill, you're probably not going to do too well. If possible, you want to send your I-messages at a time when your parents are in a good mood, feeling relaxed and unhurried, and will be more receptive to you. You could even start by asking if it's a good time to talk. Of course, it's not always possible to pick your time. Sometimes situations, conflicts, and problems come up and have to be dealt with right on the spot. But, when you have a choice, think about your timing.

Look back over Exercise #7. Did you have any control over the timing? If so, could your timing have been better?

☐ **3.** *Was there a problem with my body language or tone of voice?*

Body language says a lot. Tensing up, turning away, slouching down, pointing a finger, shaking a fist are all examples of body language. Body language and tone of voice have a lot to do with how we send our messages and how others react to what we say. We may send a perfectly lovely I-message that falls flat on its face because of our body language or tone of voice. Try to be aware of how your body language and tone of voice affects your messages.

Think back over the situation you described in Exercise #7. Was there something in your body language or tone of voice that caused your attempt to use I-messages to fail?

☐ **4.** *Did I get hooked in by my parents' you-messages?*

This is a very common problem. You've sent your parents this perfectly wonderful I-message and what do they do? They come back with a you-message! You get hooked in and before you know it, you're back in the old fight cycle of tossing you-messages back and forth at each other.

If you find that your attempts at using I-messages somehow just wind up back in the old you-message fight cycle, it may be because you're getting hooked into your parents' you-messages. Try to stay with your I-messages. Also, be sure to read the section on Active Listening below which will teach you a way of responding to your parents' you-messages without getting hooked into sending a you-message back.

Look at Exercise #7 again. Did your parents respond to your I-message with a you-message? If so, did this hook you in? Did you wind up responding to their you-message with a you-message of your own?

☐ **5.** *Did my parents attack, make fun of, deny, or in some other way put down the feelings I expressed?*

This can be a real problem. When we use I-messages instead of you-messages, we're telling the other person how we feel. If the other person attacks, makes fun of, denies, or in some other way puts our feelings down, we may be very hurt and angry.

If you have used an I-message to explain how you feel and you get one of these kinds of lines back:

"I don't care how you feel."

"It's just plain silly to feel that way."

"You shouldn't feel that way."
"Well, isn't that just too darned bad."
"How do you think I feel?"
"All you care about are your own feelings."
"Don't you dare talk to me about how angry you are."
"I'm tired of hearing your complaints."
"If you feel that way, it's your problem."
"It's stupid to feel that way."

you probably won't feel very good. In fact, you may feel so angry or hurt that you respond with a you-message.

If you have this kind of problem when you use I-messages, try not to let your feelings get in the way. Try to stick with your I-messages. The next section will teach you some reflective listening skills that will help you respond to your parents' you-messages without sending a you-message back.

Almost every parent will respond to an I-message with a put-down of the feeling being expressed once in awhile. They're only human. But, we should warn you that there are a few parents who just won't or can't respond to I-messages without ridiculing, attacking, denying, or somehow putting you down. You can try until you're blue in the face, but his kind of parent won't change. If you have this problem, you may need to read the section "Getting Help" (see pp. 145–152).

☐ **6. *Am I willing to try again?***
We hope so. But, before you have another go at it, try reading this next section, which has some ideas that may help your next attempt at using I-messages go a little more smoothly.

3: RECEIVING THE MESSAGE

So far, we've been talking about the first part of communication, that is, about *sending* the message. By now, you know the difference between I-messages and you-messages. You have a pretty good idea of how the way you send your message can help avoid fights and solve problems between you and your parents. You know how I-messages can sometimes save the day.

Now, we're going to talk about the second part of communication, that is, about *listening*, or *receiving*, the message. We're going to show you how the way you *listen* can also help avoid fights and solve problems. (We know it sounds crazy, but stay with us. Learning how to listen can work wonders!)

QUIZ

You may already know something about how to listen. Or, maybe you don't, but we're willing to bet that you know a lot about how *not* to listen. Take this two-part quiz and find out.

Part One: If your parents have ever said any of the following things (or something similar) to you, put an *X* in front of that statement.

☐ "Pay attention when I'm speaking to you!"

☐ "Don't pretend you don't hear me!"

103

☐   "You aren't listening to a word I'm saying!"

☐   "Sit still and listen to what I'm saying!"

☐   "Take that look off your face!"

☐   "Don't interrupt me when I'm talking to you!"

☐   "Listen to me when I'm talking to you, young lady!"

☐   "Wipe that smirk off your face!"

☐   "Don't you dare take that attitude with me!"

☐   "I am *talking* to you!"

☐   "Don't act like you don't know what in the world I'm talking about!"

☐   "Look at me when I'm speaking to you!"

☐   "Don't do that when I'm trying to talk to you!"

☐   "You could at least act like you're listening when I'm talking to you!"

☐   "Earth to daughter, come in please." (Truly witty parents will say this line in a radio-transmitter or computer-like voice.)

Part Two: When your parents are talking to you, especially if they're on your case about something, do you ever . . . (*put a check mark in front of the things you might do*).

☐ **1.** Ignore them or pretend you don't hear them.

☐ **2.** Fidget, shift your body about, bob from foot to foot like small boys needing to go to the bathroom.

☐ **3.** Stare off into the distance or over your parent's shoulder.

☐ **4.** Look anywhere, except right at them.

☐ **5.** Drum your fingers or tap your toes.

☐ **6.** Cross your arms in front of your chest and assume a you-can't-tell-me-anything stance.

☐ **7.** Hunch your shoulders, slouch down, or turn away.

☐ **8.** Sigh loudly or breathe in and out noisily and slowly as if you can barely put up with it all.

☐ **9.** Take a deep breath and hold it.

☐ **10.** Smirk.

☐ **11.** Clench your teeth and grimace.

☐ **12.** Act like you're not really there.

☐ **13.** Put your hands over your ears.

☐ **14.** Do anything you can do to let them know you aren't really listening.

Comments on These Quizzes

If you don't have any check marks in these two quizzes, you're either the world's most unusual kid or not very honest.

If you have even a few check marks, you probably know a whole lot about how *not* to listen.

If you've checked a lot or *all* of the boxes, you're like most kids and you're truly an expert in how *not* to listen.

Three Steps to Improving Your Listening Skills

After taking these quizzes, it's no doubt dawned on you that you know a lot about how *not* to listen. In fact, you probably have a whole bagful of "not-listening" tricks and tactics that you use on your parents. As you know, these "not-listening" tricks and tactics work very well if you want to get your parents mad at you. In fact, they're practically 100 percent foolproof.

These tricks make it seem that you don't think what's being said is worth listening to. And maybe you don't. You may be saying to yourself, "So, why should I have to act like I do?" The answer is that you don't *have* to pay attention when your parents talk to you. But, if you're trying to avoid fights and problems, you'll have much better luck if you at least *act* like you think what your parents are saying is worth listening to.

By paying attention, you're letting your parents know that you *accept* the fact that they have a right to whatever feeling or opinion it is that they're expressing. Having what we say accepted is tremendously important to most of us. Think about it. Don't you hate it when someone judges your feelings and opinions and acts as if you don't even have the right to your own thoughts and feelings?

Now, this doesn't mean that you have to act like you *agree* with what your parents are saying. Chances are that you won't *agree* with the feeling or opinion they're expressing, especially if they're chewing you out or are on your case about something. You may not like what they're saying, not one little bit. You may not feel that their opinion or feeling is justified. You may, in fact, think they're dead wrong! No way are we suggesting that you should act like you agree if you don't!

But, even if you don't *agree* with what your parents are saying, you can *accept* the fact that they have a right to their own feelings and opinions. If you can learn to communicate acceptance and understanding to your parents, we think you'll be amazed at how much easier your life will be.

In the next several pages, we'll be teaching you three steps which will help you improve your listening skills so that you can avoid fights and begin to solve problems and conflicts between you and your parents. Steps One and Two are pretty easy. Step Three is ... well, it's a little trickier. But, once you've learned these three steps and how to use them, we think you'll find that you'll be able to avoid at least some of the storms that usually go on between parents and their preteen or teenage children.

HOW TO LISTEN: STEP ONE

Step One in our three-part program for learning how to listen is pretty easy. In fact, if you know how *not* to listen, then you already know Step One. Step One is simply to do the opposite of "not listening."

In other words, Step One means doing things like keeping quiet, not interrupting, standing or sitting still, looking your parents in the eye, using your body language to show that you're tuned in, and so forth. In short, it means paying attention.

Being quiet, paying attention, looking your parents in the eye, using body language to show you are listening, you are usng what psychologists call *passive* listening skills. "Passive" means just the opposite of "active." With passive listening, you don't have to do much of anything. You just stand there and act like you are listening.

Step 1: Passive Listening   Step 2: Active Listening

Passive listening and Active listening.   Shown left, passive listening employs body language—especially eye-contact—to communicate that you're listening. The next step is active listening: grunt, nod, say things that will encourage the speaker to say more.

HOW TO LISTEN: STEP TWO

Now that you've learned how Step One can help you communicate acceptance and understanding to your parents, you are ready for Step Two. It sounds easy, doesn't it? It is and it can go a long way toward preventing fights with your parents. Step Two in learning how to listen is also pretty easy. In fact, you already know this tactic, too.

In Step Two, you do what psychologists call active listening. The active listening of Step Two requires a little bit more (but not much more) work on your part than the passive listening of Step One. The following quiz will help you recognize the times when you already use active listening skills.

QUIZ

When your parents are talking to you, do you ever say or do any of the following things? Put an *X* in front of each of these active listening skills that you've used.

☐ **1.** Acknowledge by nodding or cocking your head to the side so that your parents know that you are listening and to go on talking.

☐ **2.** Make simple sounds or say short words such as, "Uh-huh," "Hmmm," "So . . .," or "And . . ." to let your parents know you *are* listening and that you're willing to hear more.

☐ **3.** Say things like, "Really!" "You're kidding!" "You don't say so!" to give your parents the idea that you're tuned in to what they're saying.

☐ **4.** As your parents speak, encourage them by using simple phrases such as "that's interesting" or "never thought of that" so it can lead up to a two-way conversation.

☐ **5.** Ask questions like "How do you feel about that?" "What exactly do you mean?" or "What happened next?" to get your parents to go on with what they're saying.

YOUR SCORE

If you've checked even one box, you *do* know how to use Step Two, active listening skills.

If you've checked more than one or *all* boxes, you're pretty good at using these active listening skills.

If you haven't checked any, you might want to start trying some of these things. It's really not very difficult and it can have a big effect on your parents.

Active listening of this type encourages the other person to talk, and tells the other person that he or she is being heard, that you're interested, that you accept his or her right to feel or think whatever it is he or she is telling you. After all, you're listening, aren't you? Active listening can work wonders!

HOW TO LISTEN: STEP THREE

Steps One and Two—that is, paying attention, looking your parents in the eye, and not interrupting; and saying things like "Go on" or "Tell me more"—tell your parents that you are listening, that you think what they're saying is worth hearing, and that you're willing to hear more. Step Three is a way of showing your parents that you *truly* understand and accept what they're saying.

Step Three is another active listening skill called mirror listening or *reflective* listening, because when you use this skill you become a mirror, reflecting back what has been said to you.

Different psychologists have different names for this skill, as well as their own

Reflective Listening. Begin by saying something like "I guess you're feeling..." or "Sounds like you're feeling..."

Then, "fill in the feeling." Use a feeling word or phrase that describes what you think the other person is feeling.

---

reflective (re-FLECK-tiv)

handy tips on how to use it. But we think the best advice—at least the best for kids—is found in Alex J. Packer's book *Bringing Up Parents:* You can't just repeat or parrot back *exactly* what's been said; in order for reflective listening to work really well, you have to reflect back the *feeling* behind your parent's words.

It's not always easy to figure out what another person is feeling and to reflect back what they're feeling. But, if you can learn to do so, you'll find that it's a skill you can use to avoid fights and to begin solving problems between you and your parents.

Perhaps the best way to explain reflective or mirror listening is to give you a few examples.

EXAMPLE #1

Mother: (Coming in the door) Young lady, you get off the phone this instant! I've been trying to call home for the last two hours, but I couldn't get through because you were on the phone. How many times have I told you not to tie up the phone like that! You just never listen, do you? Well, your telephone privileges are suspended. You're not to use the phone for a whole month!

Suppose that the daughter had made one of the more usual or typical responses that a kid in this situation might make:

- "It's not my fault. How was I supposed to know you were trying to call?"

- "If you'd let me have my own phone, this wouldn't happen."

- "Well, *you're* always tying up the phone talking to *your* friends."

If the daughter had said one of these things (or something along these lines), the mother probably would have gotten even madder than she already was. In fact, these typical responses probably would have started a major fight.

Now, let's see how things might have gone once the daughter used reflective listening.

Daughter: Wow, it must have been really, really frustrating for you to have called and gotten a busy signal. *(Daughter doesn't respond to the you-messages the mother is sending. Instead, the daughter uses reflective listening. She identifies the feeling, in this case frustration, behind the mother's words.)*
Mother: You bet it was! I called before I left the office. Busy! I stopped at the grocery store and called from the phone booth. Busy! I stopped to get gas and called from the station. Still busy!!!

Daughter: You must have felt like killing me! *(Daughter again reflects back the feeling.)*

Mother: I sure did! Who on earth were you talking to for so long? *(Mother cools down enough to ask a question.)*

Daughter: I was talking to Sally. I didn't realize how long I was on. We have a math test tomorrow and she was explaining some of it to me. I guess we were also just yakking. *(Daughter gets a chance to explain.)*

Mother: Well, something's got to change, because sometimes I need to reach you by phone on my way home from work. I wanted to tell you to take the chicken out of the freezer. Now there won't be time for the chicken to defrost before dinner.

Daughter: Maybe we could have that leftover casserole, and maybe from now on I could stay off the phone 'till you're home. *(They're on their way to thinking up ways to solve the problem instead of fighting.)*

Reflective listening turned what could have been a you-message fight into a situation where the parent and daughter could begin to solve their problems.

EXAMPLE #2

Father: I lent you my tools to build your science project, and you left them lying out there in the back yard. Now it's rained and they're getting all rusty. Don't ever ask to borrow my things again!

Typical responses that a daughter might make in this kind of situation are:

- "It's not my fault. I didn't know it was going to rain."

- "I meant to pick them up, I just forgot. Can't a person ever make a mistake around here without you acting like it's the end of the world?"

- "Well, I don't ever want to use your precious tools again anyhow. So there!"

As you know, these sorts of responses are probably going to start a major fight. Let's see how using reflective listening instead of these typical responses could work in this example.

Daughter: I guess you're feeling like I was pretty inconsiderate and that I treated you awfully unfairly. *(This father is mad. He's also feeling that he's been treated in an unfair and inconsiderate manner. The daughter uses reflective listening to let the father know she accepts and understands what he is saying.)*

Father: That's right. You are so inconsiderate and irresponsible. Those tools are practically ruined!

Daughter: You must be really frustrated and disappointed. Your tools are really important to you. (*Daughter again uses reflective listening.*)

Father: Yes, they are, and now I won't be able to use them. Just what do you plan to do about it, young lady? (*Father has cooled down enough to ask a question.*)

Daughter: Maybe I could use some steel wool and oil to get them back into shape. (*Daughter gets a chance to suggest a solution to the problem.*)

Father: Well, maybe that will work. (*Father is cooling off.*)

Daughter: If I can't fix them, maybe I could buy replacements out of my allowance money. (*Daughter suggests another solution.*)

Father: Well, as long as you use steel wool and oil, I think they'll be okay. (*The father and daughter agree on a solution. A major fight is avoided.*)

EXAMPLE #3

Mother: I work hard all day long, and I come home to find that you haven't done any of the things I asked you to do. You knew we were having company for dinner tonight and that I had to work late. All I asked was that you spend a few minutes straightening up the living room. You want me to do things for you, but you won't lift a finger to help me out.

Again, the typical responses are:

- "Well, it's *your* company that's coming for dinner, why should *I* have to clean up for *your* friends!"

- "How come I'm the one who has to do all the housework. Why don't you ask Jimmy (your younger brother). He never has to do anything around here."

- "I didn't have time to do it. I had too much homework."

Here again, all those typical responses will only make the mother angrier. Let's see how reflective listening might work better.

Daughter: You must be feeling like everything falls to you. I guess you think I'm awfully unfair, that I've really been selfish. (*Again, the daughter becomes a mirror and reflects back the feeling behind the mother's words.*)

Mother: I sure do, and I'm sick and tired of it. I can only do so much.

Daughter: You hoped I'd pitch in and help out and you're disappointed that I didn't come through for you. (*Daughter again reflects the feeling behind the mother's words.*)

Mother: Yes, I am. But, I'd still like it if you'd do it right now. (*Mother is less angry and thinks up a solution to the problem.*)

Daughter: O.K. I'll have this place cleaned up in a jiffy. (*Again, a solution to the problem is found and a major fight has been avoided.*)

Remember the parent and daughter who had the fight about coming home late? The daughter walked in the door two hours late and the parent said, "Young lady, where have you been? You were supposed to be home at ten o'clock and it's past midnight! You just can't be trusted can you?"

What was the parent feeling in this situation? Anger? Sure, there was anger, but anger is usually a mask for a deeper feeling. A person may be angry because he or she feels hurt, cheated, betrayed, confused, guilty, foolish, or half a dozen other things. Here, chances are the feeling under the anger—in fact, the feeling that *caused* the anger—was worry. The parent was *worried* about the daughter's safety.

Let's see how reflective listening might have worked in this situation:

Daughter: Sounds like you've been really worried about me. (*Daughter identifies underlying feeling and uses reflective listening to reflect the feeling back to the parent.*)

Parent: I'll say I've been worried. I've been half out of my mind with worry. What happened? (*Parent stops sounding angry and asks a question.*)

Daughter: Susan's car broke down. We walked to the gas station and got someone to help us. I tried to call, but the phone booth was out of order. I'm really sorry. (*Daughter gets a chance to explain.*)

Parent: Well, I'm glad to hear that you tried to call. And, the important thing is that you're home safe and sound! (*A fight is avoided.*)

HOW TO USE REFLECTIVE LISTENING

After reading these examples, you probably have a better idea of how reflective, or mirror, listening works and how it can help avoid fights and solve problems. Now you're ready to learn how *you* can put reflective listening to work for you.

In the book *Bringing Up Parents*, author Alex J. Packer suggests that when you want to use reflective listening, it's best to start by saying something like:

"You sound as if ..."
"Sounds as if you're feeling ..."
"I bet you're feeling ..."

"Are you feeling ..."
"Are you saying that ..."
"Did you feel ..."
"You mean that ..."
"Did you mean that ..."
"I guess that makes you feel ..."

Then, fill in the feeling. Or, as authors Adele Faber and Elaine Mazlish put it, "Give the feeling a name." In other words, use a feeling word or phrase that you think reflects what your parent is feeling. Here's a list of just a few of the feeling words and phrases you might find to "fill in" or "name" the feeling when you're using reflective listening:

angry	bugged
frustrated	confused
uncertain	all alone
treated unfairly	treated unjustly
like a fool	afraid
like a jerk	worried
disappointed	unhappy
unappreciated	overburdened
taken advantage of	ripped off
full of hate	tempted to give up
that I've been selfish	doubtful
that I've been inconsiderate	that I've been (whatever)
mad	irritated
resentful	unsure
rejected	cheated
stumped	stuck
defeated	fearful
hurt	silly
insulted	sad
put upon	enraged
outraged	hateful
ignored	that I've been rude
unloved	at your wit's end

EXERCISE #1

The tricky part of reflective listening is trying to figure out the feeling behind the words. This exercise will give you some practice in naming the feeling. Read each of the comments below and fill in the feeling.

1. *Parent:* "You never want to do anything with your family anymore. You're always off with your friends."
This parent is feeling _____.

2. *Parent:* "You borrowed my sweater, and now it has chocolate milkshake stains all over it."
This parent is feeling _____.

3. *Parent:* "You never lift a finger around this house. You don't do a lick of housework unless I start yelling."
This parent is feeling _____.

4. *Parent:* "You were supposed to come right home after school. I called from work and you weren't home. You just can't be trusted, can you?"
This parent is feeling _____.

5. *Parent:* "It's bedtime and your homework isn't done! You've been watching TV all evening. You won't do a thing unless I stand over you and watch you the whole time."
This parent is feeling _____.

6. *Parent:* "If I've told you once, I've told you a hundred times, keep our stereo turned down. We can't even hear ourselves think. But, you never listen, do you? If I ask you nicely, you ignore me. I have to scream at you before you pay any attention at all."
This parent is feeling _____.

7. *Parent:* "You are so moody and unpredictable! Last week you interrupted me while I was doing my taxes because you *had* to ask my advice about your problem with your boyfriend. Now today, when I have time and ask you about it, you tell me to stop being so nosey and go stamping off to your bedroom. What is it with you, anyhow?"
This parent is feeling _____.

8. *Parent:* "You haven't touched a thing on your plate! I cook a nice meal and you tell me you're on a diet and don't want to eat anything."
This parent is feeling _____.

9. *Parent:* "You keep asking me what topic you should pick for your term paper. But, every time I give you an idea, you say that my idea is stupid or boring or just no good. You're just impossible to deal with! I'm not even going to bother to try helping you anymore."
This parent is feeling _____.

10. *Parent:* "I spent a lot of money buying you that new outfit. You said you loved it. But, now I see that it's hanging in the back of your closet and you've never worn it once. Do you think money grows on trees?"
This parent is feeling _____.

SAMPLE ANSWERS FOR EXERCISE #1

Words like *angry, bugged, pissed off, furious,* and *mad* would probably work for most or all of these situations. But, in the sample answers below, we've tried to use words or phrases that get at the deeper feeling beneath the words. Your answers may not be the same as ours. In fact, you may have come up with better answers than we have. But, we've included these sample answers to give you some idea of how to identify the underlying feeling.

1. This parent is, of course, angry and mad. But, beneath the anger, this parent may be feeling ignored, unimportant to you, sad, like you don't care about him or her anymore, that you don't enjoy spending time with him or her. This parent may even be feeling a bit jealous.

2. Here again, this parent is angry. In fact, this parent may even be furious or enraged. But, underneath the fury, this parent is feeling ripped off, taken advantage of, resentful, treated unfairly or unjustly, or that you've been inconsiderate, selfish or uncaring.

3. Once again, angry, mad, furious and similar words will work here. Beneath these angry feelings this parent is probably feeling that s/he has been treated unfairly or unjustly, that you've been inconsiderate, rude or uncaring, that everything falls to him or her, or that you don't really care about his or her feelings. Other words that might be good answers include *overburdened, cheated, ripped off, resentful, frustrated,* or *ignored.*

4. Sure, this parent is mad or even downright furious. But why? Underneath the anger, this parent was probably feeling worried, concerned, scared or afraid.

5. In addition to anger, this parent may be feeling frustrated, resentful, disappointed, put upon, asked to do more than his or her share, overburdened, hopeless, or tempted to give up on you.

6. Besides being hopping mad, this parent may be feeling taken advantage of, treated unfairly, at their wit's end, defeated, resentful, frustrated, or hopeless. This parent may also be feeling that you've been inconsiderate, rude or selfish.

7. *Confused, uncertain, disappointed, rejected, ignored, tempted to give up, stuck, stumped*—these sorts of words would be good ones in this situation.

8. This parent is, no doubt, mad that you're not eating your dinner. This parent may also be worried or concerned about your not eating and your dieting all the time. Along with this, a parent in this situation may be feeling unappreciated, frustrated or otherwise upset because you won't eat the meal he or she has gone to the trouble of making.

9. Once again, we've got a parent who's mad and angry. But, underneath the anger, this parent is feeling put down, rejected, ignored, frustrated, insulted, hurt, unappreciated and probably half a dozen other things as well.

10. There's no doubt that this parent is angry about spending money for something you won't wear. But, besides feeling angry, this parent is probably confused, uncertain or unsure about why you don't like the outfit anymore. This parent may also be feeling rejected or hurt. Words like *frustrated* or *resentful* might also describe what this parent is feeling.

EXERCISE #2

Okay, now that you've had some practice identifying the feeling behind the words, you're ready to try your newly learned reflective listening skills on your parents.

The next time one of your parents is bugged, mad, angry, on your case, or chewing you out, try using reflective listening. Then use the blank space to write a brief description of what happened and answer the questions below.

_____

_____

_____

_____

_____

_____

1. What was your parent mad or angry about?

_____

_____

2. What exactly (or as close as you can remember) did your parent say when he or she was getting on your case?

_____

_____

_____

3. Did you use reflective listening? If so, tell exactly what you said (or as close as you can remember). If you weren't able to use reflective listening, explain why not._____

_____

_____

4. How did your parent react when you used reflective listening? What did he or she say or do?_____

_____

_____

_____

5. Were you happy with the way things turned out? Did reflective listening do the job for you? Did it help you to avoid a fight or to solve your problem? If not, what do you think went wrong?_____

_____

_____

_____

_____

COMMENTS ON EXERCISE #2

If you tried reflective listening and it worked well for you—congratulations! You'll probably want to go on using reflective listening in other situations.

If you tried reflective listening and it didn't work so well, you may be thinking that it's just a waste of time. Or, if you tried reflective listening and your attempt seemed silly, fell flat on its face, or made matters worse (all of which *can* happen), chances are you're ready to throw this book in the trash!

But, please don't give up yet! Reflective listening is probably something new for you. Like all new things, it takes a little getting used to. It may feel weird or awkward at first. You may get it right the first time. You may have a little trouble (or even a whole lot!) your first time. You may make mistakes or even fall flat on your face.

There are very few people in this world who can try something new and do it perfectly well on the first try. Earlier, we asked you to think about what happened the first time you tried to ride a bike. Did you just hop on the bike and go pedaling merrily along? No way! Well, in some ways learning to use reflective listening is like learning to ride a bike. You've got to try and try again before you get good at it.

But before you try again, we'd like you to read through the following section, "Common Problems in Using Reflective Listening." In fact, even if your first attempt at using reflective listening worked pretty well, we'd still like you to read through this next section. Knowing about these common problems will help you in your future attempts at using reflective listening.

COMMON PROBLEMS IN
USING REFLECTIVE LISTENING

If you had problems in your first attempt to use reflective listening in Exercise #2, some of the problems on this list may sound familiar to you. If so, we'd like you to put a check mark in the appropriate box and to pay particular attention to that problem, so you can avoid it in your next attempt at using reflective listening.

If things went pretty well in your first attempt at using reflective listening, you still might find that one or more of the items on the list sounds like a problem that might possibly come up in your future attempts. If so, put a check mark in front of the item so that you'll be better able to deal with the problem if it comes up in your future attempts at using reflective listening.

☐ **1.** *Using the wrong word or words to name the feeling.* This is a very common problem. Most of us just aren't very used to naming the feeling behind another person's words. As a result, we sometimes get the feeling wrong or use too weak or too strong a word to reflect the feeling. Moreover, people often mask or hide their real feelings, and this too makes it difficult to name the underlying feeling.

Using the wrong word(s) to name the feeling isn't always a problem. For instance, we may say something like, "Sounds like you're feeling angry," when actually the other person isn't angry, but is feeling confused or hurt or some other way. The other person may simply say, "No, I'm not angry, I'm just confused."

But, sometimes getting the feeling wrong can cause problems. For example:

Daughter: Sounds like you're feeling confused.
Mother: Don't you tell me I'm confused young lady! I'm not one bit confused!
I'll tell you who's confused around here. You're the one who's confused.
If you think I'm going to put up with this kind of behavior from you, young lady, you are sadly confused. You are sadly mistaken. I'm not . . .

This daughter's mistake in naming the feeling really set this mother off. Luckily, this kind of thing is easily cured. All you need to do is to correct yourself. In the above example, the daughter could have said something like, "I guess confused wasn't a very good word. I guess what you're really feeling is angry, huh?"

If you don't get the feeling right, don't let it throw you. Correct yourself and start again. Keep using reflective listening until you do get the feeling right!

☐ **2.** *Using reflective listening at the wrong time or in the wrong situation.* Reflective listening is a tool, a communication tool. Like all tools, it works well for doing some jobs and not so well for others. Your common sense will tell you that for doing a job like, for instance, unscrewing a screw, you need to use a screwdriver, not a hammer or a saw. You need to use a little common sense with reflective listening, too.

Reflective listening works well in situations where your parent wants to have his or her feelings heard and accepted. In other situations, reflective listening just isn't the right tool. For example, suppose your mom says, "Hurry up and get your books and get out the door. The school bus is waiting!"

Is this a situation for reflective listening? No way! Your mom doesn't want to hear you say, "Gee mom, it sounds like you're really concerned that I might miss the bus." Your mom wants action. She wants you to get your act together and get out the door—*fast!*

☐ **3.** *Using a you-message instead of reflective listening.* Sometimes, even though we may be trying to use reflective listening, what we end up doing instead is sending a you-message. Suppose, for example, your dad is feeling uptight. If you say, "Gee, you must be feeling uptight," or "Sounds like you're feeling uptight," you'd be using reflective listening. But, if you said, "You're really uptight," your comments could sound like a blaming, accusing you-message.

If your attempts at reflective listening end up sounding like you-messages, try to remember to put your reflective listening comments in question form. For instance, you might ask your parent, "Are you feeling uptight?" This will help get you out of the you-message trap and get you on the right track with reflective listening.

☐ **4.** *Giving up too soon.* Sometimes we may start out using reflective listening, but we give up too soon. Instead of staying with reflective listening, we switch over to you-messages. Before we know it, we're back into a full-scale you-message fight. It's easy to have this happen because your parents will often respond to reflective listening with you-messages. Look at what happened between this mother and daughter. The mother was on the daughter's case for being on the phone too long.

Daughter: I guess you're really annoyed with me for tying up the phone. (*Daughter uses reflective listening.*)
Mother: I sure am. I'm expecting a call and you've been on that phone for over an hour. Can't you ever have any consideration for others?
Daughter: Well, you don't have to yell. You're always yelling at me for every little thing. (*Daughter forgets about reflective listening. She gives up and starts using you-messages.*)
Mother: Don't you take that attitude with me, young lady! And, you stay off that phone for the rest of the evening!

If the daughter had been able to stay with reflective listening instead of falling back on you-messages, things might have gone a bit better for her.

Daughter: I guess you're really annoyed with me for tying up the phone.
Mother: I sure am. I'm expecting a call and you've been on the phone for over an hour. Can't you ever have any consideration for others?

Daughter: Sounds like you feel that I've been awfully inconsiderate. (*Daughter doesn't hook in to the mother's you-message. She doesn't give up; she keeps using reflective listening.*)

Mother: Yes, I do and you have been! How can I get my call with you on the phone like that? (*Mother is still mad, but instead of getting madder and telling the daughter she can't use the phone for the rest of the evening, the mother asks a question.*)

Daughter: I guess you couldn't very well get your call with me tying up the phone. How 'bout if I stay off the phone until you've gotten your call? (*Daughter gets to suggest a solution to the problem.*)

Mother: Yes, please stay off until then. You can use the phone again once I've gotten my call. (*A major blowup is avoided.*)

It may be difficult to stay with reflective listening, especially if your parent is sending you-messages. But, if you can hang in there and stay with reflective listening, you've got a much better chance of having things go your way.

☐ *5. Expecting too much of reflective listening.* "I used reflective listening and it didn't work," one teenager complained to us. "My dad was still mad."

This daughter had made a very common mistake. She expected too much of reflective listening. She thought that simply because she used reflective listening, her dad was all of a sudden going to stop being mad. Reflective listening doesn't make feelings disappear. If, for instance, your parent is hopping mad, you can use reflective listening until you're blue in the face, but your parent is still going to be mad. However, reflective listening can usually keep your parent from getting any madder, and as you know, this alone can mean a lot.

Don't expect reflective listening to solve your problems, either. It's true that reflective listening can often pave the way and put you on the road to solving your problems, but it's not a cure-all. Sometimes, you and your parents will need more than just reflective listening. To learn about other ways of dealing with your problems, read the next section—on problem solving.

4: SOLVING
PROBLEMS

If you've gotten this far and have read the information, taken the quizzes, and done the exercises in Sections 2 and 3, you're now an expert (well, *almost* an expert) at communicating. You've learned some new communication skills. For instance, you know the difference between you-messages and I-messages. You know about reflective listening. You know how using I-messages and reflective listening can help avoid fights and conflicts.

You've also seen how these communication skills of I-messages and reflective listening can start you and your parents on the road to solving your problems. Now, you're ready to put these communication skills to work in solving your problems with your parents in a new way!

The "No-Lose" Method

The new way of solving problems that we'll be talking about in this section is called the "win/win" or "no-lose" method of solving problems. Psychologists use these terms for the simple reason that when problems are solved by this method, everybody wins and nobody loses.

Now, we have to admit that this all may sound like a lot of confusing double talk! But, if you'll hang in there just a little bit longer we think we'll be able to make it all a bit less confusing.

THE "WIN/LOSE" METHOD

Let's begin by talking about what happens when kids and parents have a fight. Many families, many people for that matter, use the win/lose method of solving problems. The parent "wins" the fight and the kid "loses;" or the kid "wins" and the parent "loses." In the dialogue below, there are two examples of a conflict between a parent and a teenage daughter. Can you tell who wins and who loses?

Daughter: I'm going to the football game tonight.
Parent: Be sure you're home by eleven o'clock.
Daughter: Eleven o'clock! The game's not over till ten or ten thirty, and then everyone's going out for pizza.
Parent: You know the rules. It's an eleven o'clock curfew on Friday nights.
Daughter: Everyone else's parents lets them stay out till midnight or one.
Parent: I don't care what everyone else's parents do. Your curfew is eleven o'clock. I want you home by then.
Daughter: But that's not fair. You always treat me like a baby.
Parent: Don't talk to me in that tone of voice, young lady.
Daughter: But I ...
Parent: No buts about it. Either you're home by eleven or you don't go!
Daughter: (Angrily) Oh, all right. I'll be home by eleven.

In this example, do you think the parent wins (child loses) or the child wins (parent loses)?_____.

Daughter: I'm going to the football game tonight.
Parent: Be sure you're home by eleven o'clock.
Daughter: Eleven o'clock! The game's not over till ten or ten thirty, and then everyone's going out for pizza.
Parent: You know the rules. It's an eleven o'clock curfew on Friday nights.
Daughter: Everyone else's parents lets them stay out till midnight or one.
Parent: I don't care what everyone else's parents do. Your curfew is eleven o'clock. I want you home by then.
Daughter: But, that's not fair. You always treat me like a baby.
Parent: I'm not being unfair. Eleven o'clock is late enough.
Daughter: Well, if you won't let me stay out, then I just won't go to the game.
Parent: Now, honey, you know we want you to go out and have fun with your friends.
Daughter: Well, then, let me stay out till one. I'm not a kid any more. You always treat me like a baby. If you don't let me stay out, I'll run away from home.
Parent: Oh, I give up. Stay out if you want. I don't want to argue with you any more. You never listen to a thing I say anyhow.

Who do you think was the winner in this situation? As you've probably guessed, in the first conflict the parent won; in the second, the daughter did.

Most families solve problems by the win/lose method.

Either the parents win   *Or the kid wins*
and the kid loses ...   *and the parents lose.*

But, there is another way! When family problems are solved by the win/ win or no-lose method. When problems are solved by this method, everybody wins and nobody loses.

HOW DOES YOUR FAMILY SOLVE PROBLEMS?

In some families problems are solved by having the parents always win or almost always and the kids lose. In others, usually or often the kids win, while the parents lose. In still other families, parents and the kids go back and forth, taking turns winning and losing. A few lucky families solve their problems through an entirely different method, the "win/win," or "no-lose" method, in which everybody wins and nobody loses.

We'd like you to think about how fights and conflicts are settled and problems solved in your family. Since both parents don't always use the same methods we'll be asking you to answer the first question about your father and the second about your mother.

1. When I have a fight, conflict, or problem with my father ... (pick the answer that comes closest):
- **a.** He usually wins;
- **b.** I usually win;
- **c.** We take turns winning and losing;
- **d.** We work it out so neither of us wins or loses.

2. When I have a fight, conflict, or problem with my mother ... (pick the answer that comes closest):
- **a.** She usually wins;
- **b.** I usually win;
- **c.** We take turns winning and losing;
- **d.** We work it out so neither of us wins or loses.

FREEWRITING EXERCISE

How do you feel about the methods you and your parents use to settle fights and solve problems? Use the space below to freewrite about your feelings. You might want to keep these questions in mind while you're freewriting: Are you totally happy with your method(s), totally unhappy, or somewhere in between? Why do you feel the way you do? Do you feel the methods your family uses are fair to you? Why or why not? Do you think your parents feel the methods your family uses are fair to you? Why or why not?

Of course, since this is a freewriting exercise, you don't have to answer these questions. Just keep the topic of how your family solves problems in mind and start writing. Don't stop until you've filled up all the space.

_____

_____

_____

_____

_____

_____

_____

_____

_____

_____

DRAWBACKS TO THE WIN/LOSE METHOD

If your parents seem to win fights all or even just some of the time you're probably not too happy, because you're the loser, and nobody likes to lose. But even though your parents are the winners, in the long run they lose, too. Parents often end up paying a big price for winning. For one thing, when the parent wins and gets to say how the problem will be solved, the kid may not be too terrific at carrying out the solution. Kids may "forget" what they're supposed to do, drag their feet, only go through the motions, or have what is commonly known as a "bad attitude." Because the kid has lost and probably isn't too happy with the solution, the parent constantly has to be a policeman and enforce the solution. Also, problems tend to keep coming up over and over again, and even if the parents keep winning they have to pay the price of having constant fights, conflicts, and problems with their kids.

Situations when the kids always win aren't necessarily much better, although the idea might sound good to you. For one thing, kids from these families usually have to throw temper tantrums in order to win and get their own way, which isn't much fun for *anyone*. Having to deal with kids who resort to throwing tantrums isn't much fun for the parents, either. These parents often feel "jerked around," bullied, or browbeaten, and they have deeply resentful and angry feelings towards their kids. In turn, kids in these families often feel unloved. They don't think their parents care enough about them to bother putting up a fight. Here again, both the parents and kids miss out on the chance to have a loving, close relationship with one other.

Using the No-Lose Method

In this method, everybody wins. Everybody wins because everybody involved agrees on how to solve the problem.

Does this sound too good to be true? Are you having trouble believing that your family could solve problems in such a way that everyone was happy with the solution? Well, trust us. The no-lose method can and does work! This is not to say that it's easy to learn to use this method. It's not, at least not at first. But, if you're willing to work at it, we think you'll be able to learn to use this method to solve problems with your parents.

THE SIX STEPS

Each of the psychologists and authors who've written about the no-lose method explains it a little differently, but basically it involves six steps of solving problems:

Step One:	Define the problem
Step Two:	Brainstorm for solutions

Step Three: Evaluate and discuss the solutions

Step Four: Choose a solution

Step Five: Decide on a plan of action

Step Six: Follow up and evaluate

Once you and your parents have had some practice and have learned to use the no-lose method, you won't actually have to sit down and go through all six steps each time you have a problem. Eventually, the no-lose method will be so familiar that you'll be able to do it at the drop of a hat. But at first, you'll probably need to have a formal problem-solving session when disputes come up, going through all six steps, one at a time.

PROBLEM-SOLVING SESSIONS

When you're first starting to use the no-lose method, you'll want to invite your parent or parents to have a problem-solving session. Explain that you have some new ideas about how the family could avoid conflicts and that you'd like to try out these ideas. You might even read your parents some of the material in this section of the book before your first problem-solving session.

To begin with, pick a time for your session when everyone involved is feeling relaxed and unhurried. At least for the first session, you should also pick a topic ahead of time. Don't pick some general topic like the fact that your parents always treat you like a baby or never trust you. Pick a specific problem. For example, you might decide to focus on sharing the telephone, splitting household chores, getting a bigger allowance, not being allowed to stay out after ten o'clock, cleaning your room, or some other specific situation that causes conflicts, problems, or fights in your family.

Start by explaining that there are six steps to solving problems in this new way. Explain each step and lay out the ground rules before you start.

Let's take an example and look at each step closely, so you'll know how it works. In his book *Bringing Up Parents* Alex J. Packer describes a family having a problem-solving session about the use of the telephone. Since this is a common problem, we'll also use it as an example. If you'd like other examples, you might want to read *Bringing Up Parents*, which has dozens of examples of common problems and how to use problem-solving sessions to deal with these problems.

Step One: Define the Problem. At this step, the family members get to say how they see the situation that's causing the fight, conflict, or problem; how they feel about the situation; and exactly what is bothering them. There are three ground rules here:

1. Take turns so everyone has a chance to speak.
2. Don't interrupt while another person is talking.
3. Don't allow name-calling, blaming, or accusing.

Let's say that you've decided that the problem your family is going to try to solve is the use of the telephone. Step One might go something like this.

You: When I'm not allowed to use the telephone for more than a few minutes at a time, I feel really frustrated. Sometimes, I need help with my homework, and it's also really important to me to be able to just talk with my friends.

Father: I have calls I need to make. People at work sometimes need to call me at home, and if the phone's tied up, they can't get through.

Mother: I like to have the phone available, too. Besides, if you're talking on the phone, I worry that you won't do your homework. I also get irritated when you get on the phone right after dinner instead of helping with the dishes and cleaning up.

Younger Sis: You're always on the phone and then I don't get a chance. By the time you're off the phone, it's my bedtime.

Here everyone got a chance to say how he or she felt about the situation. Of course, it's likely that things won't go this smoothly during your family's first problem-solving session. Most families get stuck on Step One the first time they try to use the no-lose method. In fact, you may find that you end up having a giant you-message fight, rather than solving problems. If you think your family might have trouble with Step One, or if you try the no-lose method and run into trouble with Step One, read the section on troubleshooting on pages 135–138.

Step Two: Brainstorming for Solutions. Now that everyone has taken a position, you're ready to start brainstorming and thinking up solutions. To do this, write down all the solutions you can think up on a piece of paper. The solutions don't necessarily have to be practical ones or ones that everyone likes or agrees with. In fact, some of the solutions on your list may be totally outrageous, entirely impractical, or completely unacceptable to someone else. That's okay. In fact, sometimes, a workable solution comes out of a totally outrageous suggestion. So, just make as long a list as you can. There are two important ground rules here.

1. Everyone involved has to think up at least one solution.

2. No one can comment on anyone else's solution yet. No saying things such as, "I like it," "I don't like it," "That's not fair," "No way I'm going to do that." Just make the list.

Here's a list of sample solutions that your family might come up with if they were brainstorming about the problems of telephone use.

1. Each family member will get a separate phone.

2. Each person can use the phone as long as he or she likes. But if another person wants to use it, the user has to get off within five minutes.

3. Only younger sister can use the phone.

4. Only mom and dad can use the phone after eight o'clock.

5. Younger sister has "first dibs" on the phone until her bedtime; after that, you have first "dibs."

6. No phone calls more than five minutes long.

7. No talking on the phone till the dishes are done.

8. No talking on the phone till the homework is done.

9. No talking on the phone in the evening.

10. Younger sis and you have your own phone and you share it.

11. Your family will get "call waiting," the service from the phone company that lets you know when someone else is trying to call you.

12. Your family will take turns, so each person will have a special night to use the phone.

If your family runs into trouble with Step Two, be sure to read the section on troubleshooting on pages 135–138.

Step Three: Evaluate and Discuss the Solutions. Now you read back through the list together and discuss and evaluate the solutions. Some of the solutions will get crossed off right away because they're just not possible or practical. Others will get crossed off because one or more of the people involved in your problem-solving session won't accept them. In the process of discussing, evaluating, and crossing solutions off the list, you may well find that you think up new solutions or that you change a solution so that it is acceptable to everyone.

For example, imagine the session your family might have, using the list from step two.

You: Okay, now let's go back through the list and evaluate and discuss our solutions.

Mother: Well, I think solution #1 should be crossed off because there's no way we can afford to have three more telephone lines.

Everybody: Okay, we agree. That's not practical.

You: How about #2, which let's everyone use the phone, but a person has to get off if another person wants to use it.

Younger Sis: That sounds great, but what'll happen is that I'll want to use it and you'll say you'll get off in five minutes, but half hour later, you'll still be on.

You: Well, how about if I put my travel alarm clock by the phone? When you want to use the phone, point to the time and I'll be sure to be off in five minutes.

Younger Sis: Well, that sounds good, but what if this happens: You're using the phone, I ask you to get off in five minutes, and I get on. Five minutes later you're back again, five minutes later I'm back again.

You: You're right. I could see us doing just that. Maybe we could include the suggestion that you have first dibs before eight o'clock and I have first dibs after. That doesn't mean I can't ever use the phone before eight o'clock or you can't ever use it after eight o'clock, but we'll kind of think of "before eight" as your time and "after eight" as mine, and maybe that would keep us from interrupting each other every five minutes.

Younger Sis: Well, that might work. I'd be willing to give that a try.

Father: I'm glad you girls are working it all out. But what about me? My problem and your mother's problem is being able to get incoming phone calls.

Everybody: (Laughing) Okay.

You: I think we can cross off some of these others like #10, giving Sis and me our own phone because it would cost a lot more than call waiting. I'd like to cross off #4, which lets only Mom and Dad use the phone after eight o'clock because I'd like to be able to use the phone after eight.

Father: I'll agree to crossing those off and I think #12, which gives each of us a phone night, isn't very good either. And #9, which prevents us all from using the phone in the evening should go. Number 6, no calls over 5 minutes, doesn't seem very workable, either.

Everyone: Okay.

Mother: I'm still concerned about phone use right after dinner when the dishes aren't done. And I'm also worried that you won't do your homework.

Father: I'm still worried about being able to get calls and the phone being tied up.

You: Well, how about solution #11, that we get call waiting? That way, neither Mom or you would miss phone calls.

Father: Well, that's an idea, but who would pay for it?

You: It's not that expensive. I'd be willing to pay for part from my allowance and maybe Sis would, too. And maybe you and Mom could pay part.

Everybody: Sounds possible.

You: How about if we leave solution #11 on the list and we figure out exactly how we'll pay for it in Step Five, the plan-of-action stage. Meanwhile, can we cross #3 where only Sis can use the phone? I think we can all agree that that's not really fair if you're the only one who can use the phone.

Everybody: Yeah!

You: Suppose we said that, after dinner, neither Sis nor I could use the phone until the dishes were done and the dinner mess was cleaned up.

Mother: That would be fine, but what about your homework?

You: Well, that's a problem. Sometimes Sis and I use the phone because we're getting help with our homework. And to tell you the truth, sometimes I like to take a break from my homework by talking on the phone. I really don't think that either Sis or I don't get around to our homework because we're on the phone. Both our grades are good. If our grades started to slip, then maybe we could change the rules if that happened.

Mother: That sounds reasonable.

Here, in our example, everything has gone very smoothly, but things don't always go this smoothly in real life. If you and your family have trouble with Step Three, be sure to read the section on troubleshooting on page 135–138.

Step Four: Choose A Solution. During this step, you and your family will go back over your list and choose a solution or solutions. Then you'll write the solution down on a piece of paper. There's only one ground rule here: Everyone must agree to the solution.

Let's see how this step might go if you and your family were trying to solve a telephone use problem.

You: Okay, let's see what we've come up with. Let me sum it all up: If one of us wants to use the phone and someone else is already using it, we'll let the person know by pointing at the clock that we'll keep by the phone. We've agreed that that person will then end his or her conversation within five minutes. As a general rule, Sis and I will agree that she has first dibs before eight o'clock and I have first dibs after eight o'clock. Neither of us can pester the other one every five minutes during those times.

We'll get call waiting and figure some way of sharing the cost. That way, no one will miss an important call. Neither Sis nor I will talk on the phone after dinner until the dinner mess is cleaned up. If our grades start to slip, we'll have to change the telephone rules. Does that sound okay to everyone?

Father: Pretty much, except I think the five minutes should only apply to you and your sister. If I'm on the phone, it's usually for business reasons and I really don't want to interrupt my conversation.

Mother: I agree. I think as parents we have more of a right to the phone. After all, we pay the bills. I don't think we should have to get off the phone for you kids. Besides, the problem isn't really with your father and me talking too long. The problem really only comes up when you kids are talking too long.

You and Sis: Okay. We'll go along with that.

Once again, if you have trouble with this step, be sure to read the section on troubleshooting on page 135–138.

Step Five: Decide on a Plan of Action. Now that you've chosen a solution, you need to figure out how to put your solution into action. During this step, you'll need to answer two questions:

1. What needs to be done to carry out our solution?
2. Who is going to do it?

Let's continue with our example in which your family solves their telephone problems.

The six steps to solving problems by the no-lose method.

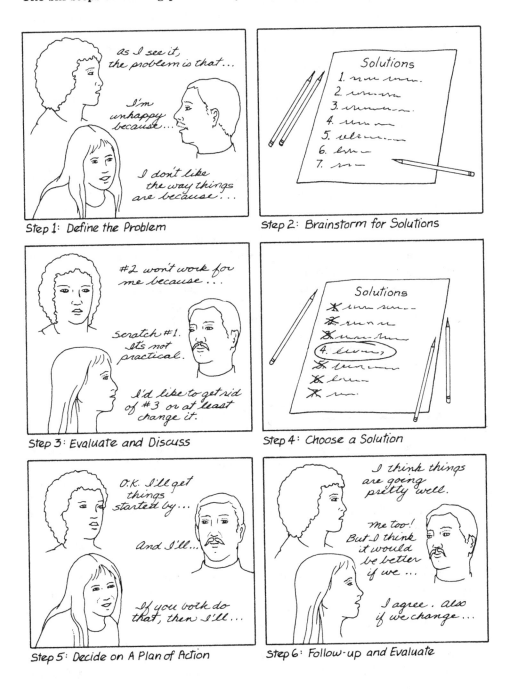

Step 1: Define the Problem

Step 2: Brainstorm for Solutions

Step 3: Evaluate and Discuss

Step 4: Choose a Solution

Step 5: Decide on A Plan of Action

Step 6: Follow-up and Evaluate

You: Okay, now that we've agreed on the solution, how are we going to put it into action? It seems to me that we need to do two things. First we have to put a clock by the phone. Then we need to call the phone company to find out how much it costs to have call waiting and if it doesn't cost too much, arrange to have it done.

Younger Sis: I'll put the clock by the phone. That's easy enough.

You: I'll call the phone company. How about this? If it costs less than ten dollars a month, I'll just go ahead and have them put call waiting on our phone service, and we can figure out how to divide the cost up later. If it's more than ten dollars, we'll have to have another meeting to figure out what to do.

Everybody: Sounds good.

If you've gotten this far in the six steps, you're well along the road to solving your problems. If, however, you run into trouble with this step, be sure to read the section on trouble-shooting.

Step Six: Follow Up and Evaluate. This step usually requires another session. After you've chosen a solution and put your plan into action, you'll need to follow up and evaluate how well your solution is working. You'll need to ask yourselves if the plan has worked. Is everyone happy with the solution you've chosen? Did you manage to get your plan into action? Do you have new problems? If so, you need to figure out what went wrong. You may need to repeat the six steps.

If your solution hasn't, for one reason or another, worked, you may need to read the material on troubleshooting.

EXERCISE #1

Now that you know the six steps to no-lose problem-solving, you're ready to put what you've learned to work for you and your family.

For this exercise, we'd like you to invite one or both of your parents to have a problem-solving session. If you think one of your parents might be more open to this new method than the other, it's probably best to ask that parent to do your first problem-solving sessions with you. However, if the problem is one that involves both parents, you'll need to do your problem-solving session with both of them.

If you have brothers or sisters or other people as part of your family, you may want to ask them to join in, too. However, since this is your first try, you might want to pick a problem involving as few people as possible. While you're first learning to solve problems in this new way, you can practice better on a smaller group.

Explain to whoever you choose to be in your first problem-solving session that you've been learning about a new way of solving problems and that you'd like them to try this new method out with you. Make sure that you pick a time that's good for everyone, that everyone's in a good mood, and that you won't be interrupted.

Begin by suggesting a specific problem you want to solve. Since this is your first try, you might want to suggest a gripe, complaint, or problem that your parent has with you, rather than one *you* have. For example, if your parent frequently gets mad at you because your bedroom is a mess, you're late for dinner, you don't do enough around the house, you talk on the phone too much, or for some other kind of behavior (or lack of action), this problem would be an excellent topic for your first session. The things that bug you—for instance, your parents not letting you date, not allowing you to go to a rock concert, making you be home by ten o'clock on weekends—are good topics for future problem-solving sessions. But, in the beginning, you'll probably find that your parents are much more willing to try this new method of problem-solving if you start by dealing with one of his or her gripes or complaints.

You might start by saying something like: "Gee, mom, I know we've had a lot of fights in the past about my bedroom being a mess. I'd like us to figure out a solution to this problem. I've been learning about a new way for parents and kids to solve their problems. I think it could work for us. Would you have time sometime soon to sit down with me and have a problem-solving session?"

Once you've set up a time and are actually getting down to business, begin by explaining or reading the six steps on page 125. You might also read through the actual description of the six steps, used in the example on pages 126–132, to give everyone an idea of what exactly is involved in this new method. You might also read the troubleshooting guide on pages 135–138 before you start, just to make sure you know what to watch out for.

After you've done this, you're ready to start with Step One. Go through each step and then write a brief description of what happened in the space below. Then answer the questions that follow.

_____

_____

_____

_____

_____

_____

1. What problem did you choose to work on for your first problem-solving session?_____

_____

_____

2. What happened in Step One, defining the problem? Did everyone get a chance to talk? If not, why not?_____

_____

_____

_____

3. If you got through Step One okay, how did Step Two, brainstorming for possible solutions, go? List all or some of the possible solutions that you all came up with._____

_____

_____

_____

4. Once you did Step Three, evaluating and discussing the solutions, did you come up with a solution in Step Four? If so, what was the solution? If not, why not?_____

_____

_____

_____

5. What plan of action, if any, did you come up with? If you weren't able to figure out a plan of action, what kept you from doing so?_____

_____

_____

_____

6. If you did manage to come up with a plan of action, how did you decide to put the plan into action? Who agreed to do what and what exactly did they agree to do?_____

_____

_____

_____

7. Did you set up a follow-up session for evaluating how well your solution and plan of action worked? If .so, when will you do this? If you didn't set up a follow-up session, why didn't you do so?_____

_____

_____

_____

8. If you did set up a follow-up session, wait until you've had that session and write about what happened. Did things work out? Did you run into problems? If so, explain those problems and how you might solve them. _____

_____

_____

_____

9. Overall, how do you think your first problem-solving session went? Are you happy with the results? Unhappy? Somewhere in between happy and unhappy? If you are happy, do you plan to try using the no-lose method to solve other problems? If you're not so happy, what do you think went wrong?_____

_____

_____

_____

Troubleshooting

The no-lose method of solving problems isn't always easy, especially at first. People can and do run into trouble. The troubleshooting guide below will help you understand and correct the difficulties you may run into in using the no-lose method of settling fights and solving problems.

If you ran into trouble trying your first excuse, you may find that something in this troubleshooting guide will help you correct what went wrong. If so, put a check mark in the appropriate box.

TROUBLESHOOTING GUIDE

☐ *Step One: Define the Problem.* This first step is sometimes the hardest. In fact, in many families, Step One leads to such a major blowout that they never, ever get to Step Two!

What goes wrong? Well, the difficulty in Step One is that when people start telling about how they see the problem, they usually use you-messages to talk about how they feel. So, one person lets loose with a blaming, accusing, attacking you-message. This, in turn, makes someone else angry or uptight, so that person interrupts or starts denying or counterattacking with a you-message. Before you know it, your problem-solving session has turned into a giant you-message fight!

(Of course, we know that *you* will be smart enough to use I-messages instead of you-messages. But, the other members of your family may not be so expert as you are, so they may use you-messages.)

If you find that Step One is turning into a you-message fight, there *are* some things you can do to get everyone back on track:

• Repeat the first two ground rules again. Remind everyone that the first ground rule is no interrupting and that the second ground rule is that everyone will get a chance to talk. Emphasize the fact that everyone *will* get a turn.

• If your family members still can't keep from interrupting each other, ask each person to write down his or her feelings about the problem on a piece of paper. Then, have each person read his or her paper aloud, while everyone else has to keep quiet.

• Remind everyone of the third ground rule for this step—no blaming, accusing, or name-calling. If your family members have trouble following this rule, add an "extra" ground rule—that everyone has to talk about his or her feelings without using the word *you* or the name of someone else in the family. This will make it impossible to use you-messages; everyone will have to use I-messages.

• Prepare your parents for this step by asking them to read some of the material in these pages on I-messages and you-messages. Or, get them a copy of Dr. Thomas Gordon's book *P.E.T.: Parent Effectiveness Training* to read. If your parents aren't the type to read a whole book, have them at least look at *How to Talk So Kids Will Listen and Listen So Kids Will Talk* by Adele Faber and Elaine Mazlish. This book has lots of cartoons that explain communication skills and the no-lose method at just a glance.

☐ *Step Two: Brainstorm for Solutions.* If you've gotten past Step One, Step Two will probably be a little easier. But families can and do run into problems with this step.

What can go wrong in Step Two? For one thing, people often start complaining about or objecting to one of the solutions someone else has suggested. Also, sometimes one or more of the people involved either *can't* think of a possible solution to suggest or *won't* offer a possible solution to the problem because they don't think they even have a chance of winning or having things go their way.

If you have these kinds of troubles with Step Two, there *are* some things you can do:

• If someone starts objecting to someone else's solution, gently remind them that this is just the brainstorming step. Discussing, evaluating, objecting to, or complaining about the solutions comes in the next step. Remind them that they will get a chance to have their say. But explain that, for now, you're just coming up with ideas and anything goes, no matter how silly, impractical, or unacceptable the idea may seem!

• If someone isn't joining in, remind the group of the ground rule for this step, that everyone is supposed to come up with at least one idea.

• If someone can't come up with something, *you* can suggest a solution for them.

• If your family is having trouble thinking up any possible solutions to the problem or if things are getting kind of uptight and tense, try adding some totally outrageous and ridiculous solutions. For example, if housework is the problem you're trying to solve, suggest that your family hire a butler or maid to do everything. As silly as that may be, write it down. Encourage everyone to think up the silliest, most ridiculous, most unworkable idea that they can imagine.

• Write down every idea that is suggested, no matter how wild or far out or terrible it seems to you.

• Don't lose your own cool. If you're having a problem-solving session with one or both your parents and one of them suggests someting that you could never, ever agree to, keep your mouth shut. Just write down the suggestion on your brainstorming list. You'll have a chance to object in the next step. All you're doing in this step is making up a list!

☐ *Step Three: Evaluate and Discuss the Solutions.* This step may sound like the hardest one yet, but if you've managed to get through Steps One and Two, you'll probably do pretty well on Step Three.

The trouble that comes up in this step is that people sometimes get offended or angry about having their suggestions vetoed or crossed off. The other big difficulty in this step is that people sometimes fall back on using you-messages. But there are things you can do to keep your problem-solving session on the right track:

• If one person objects to one of the solutions and wants to cross it off the list, but someone else objects, ask if the solution can be changed in some way so that everyone can live with it.

• Remember to use your reflective listening skills and I-messages. They will really come in handy here.

• If things get too hot and heavy, suggest that you take a break and come back to the problem-solving session later on. This will give people a chance to cool out and approach this step in a calmer manner.

☐ *Step Four: Choose A Solution.* This is not an easy step. Families may run into trouble here because the people involved just can't find a solution where everyone wins and no one loses or because one or more people involved get "talked into" accepting a solution even though they're really not happy.

If you can't find a solution that everyone agrees to, you can do one of two things:

• Suggest that you stop for now and try again later. Make sure that you set up a definite time for trying again, but don't be discouraged that you haven't found a solution right off the bat. Oftentimes, even though the first session didn't solve the problem, a second session later on *will* turn up a solution.

• Start back at Step Two again. Brainstorm again and make a new list. Repeat Step Three and have another go at Step Four.

It's also important that everyone is really and truly happy with the solution you've come up with. Check to make sure. Make a point of asking each person involved if the solution is really one they can live with. If not, keep working until you do find a compromise that satisfies everyone.

☐ *Step Five: Decide on a Plan of Action.* If you've gotten through the first four steps, you're practically home free! Things are going very well, but your troubles may not be over.

Families sometimes get messed up here because they don't really spell out the plan of action. They are so happy and excited that they've gotten this far that they sometimes forget about the practical details. Don't let this happen. Make sure that you have a plan of action and that you know how to get the wonderful solution you've all agreed on actually to work. Make sure that it clearly spells out exactly what needs to be done and exactly who's going to do it in order to make the solution work.

☐ *Step Six: Follow Up and Evaluate.* The big trouble with this step is that families sometimes forget about it—and it's important. If you don't follow up, you may find that people don't follow through on the plan of action. But, if you set a follow-up session in a few days, another week, or whenever it makes sense to do so, people will be more likely to take action on the plan. Or, if they don't, you'll know about it right away and you'll be able to get your plan back on track.

Problems can also arise when you try to put your solution to work. Having a follow-up session will ensure that you iron out any problems that may arise. In addition, by having a second session to evaluate, you'll make sure that your plan is working and that everyone is happy with the solution. And, if everything *is* going fine, you can use your follow-up session to congratulate yourself!

FREEWRITING EXERCISE

Now that we've discussed your relationship with your parents, we will turn to your relationship with your friends, with the groups that you encounter in school, and with the opposite sex. First, though, we'd like to suggest that you take a breather and reflect back on what you've read and written in this chapter. If you did in fact have a problem-solving session with your parents, did it go well? If not, why not? Perhaps you were afraid to have such a session; if so, we'd like you to think about your reasons for this, and whether they are good ones. Whatever your feelings are about what you've read in this section, it will help sort them out to take a minute and freewrite about them.

3 / YOUR SOURCES FOR GETTING HELP

1: FURTHER READING

If you have questions that weren't answered in Part One, you may find these books helpful:

1. *Changing Bodies, Changing Lives: A Book for Teens on Sex and Relationships* by Ruth Bell (New York: Random House, 1988). Absolutely the best book for teens on the topic, geared toward the fourteen-to-nineteen-year-old age group. It represents many points of view through quotes from teenagers themselves. It deals with interpersonal issues between parents and teens, and teens and peers— as well as loneliness, love, marriage, divorce, sex-role expectations, intercourse, masturbation, and other matters involving sexuality, without taking a specific stand on moral issues. There is also an excellent section on rape and incest and good information on drugs and alcohol, sexually transmitted diseases, and birth control. The section on teenage pregnancy is especially good, and the one on mental health, depression, and suicide is outstanding.

2. *Kids Need to Know* by Planned Parenthood (see address below). *Kids Need to Know* is an information kit for parents and teens. It contains the booklet "Let's Talk About ... S-E-X," by Sam Gitchel and Lorri Foster, and a number of pamphlets such as "Teen Sex?: It's OK to Say No Way" and "Basics of Birth Control." The kit is available for $10.00 (which includes postage and handling) from the Information and Education Department, Planned Parenthood, 1316 Third Street Promenade, Suite B5, Santa Monica, California 90401.

3. *Sex: A User's Manual* by The Diagram Group (New York: Berkley, 1988). Aimed at an adult audience, but presented in a well-illustrated format that teens can readily understand, this is an up-to-date guide that covers virtually every aspect of sexual experience, sexual development, and social attitudes about sex. Some conservative parents may feel uncomfortable with this book because it deals so openly with the varieties of sexual behavior. So teens will want to get permission from their parents before borrowing or buying this book.

4. *The Family Book about Sexuality* rev. ed by Mary S. Calderone, M.D., and Eric W. Johnson (New York: HarperCollins, 1990). This book is designed for the whole family. It talks about how sexuality begins when we are only tiny babies, and how it develops through puberty and adulthood. It also covers sexuality and old people. It has lots of good information about love and marriage, birth control, and sexual problems. It should be part of every family's book collection.

5. *Why Am I So Miserable If These Are the Best Years of My Life?* by Andrea Boroff Eagen (New York: Avon, 1979). Although the information on birth control and sexually transmitted diseases in this book is a bit out of date, it is still valuable for its advice to teenage girls on dealing with conflicts between parents and daughters, dating, going steady, friendships with other girls, restrictive sex roles, the double standard, making decisions about sex, saying no, being part of the "in" group, and feelings of loneliness. It has an especially good discussion about the boy-does-the-asking tradition in dating and the risks and rewards for girls who try to take the initiative.

If you'd like to learn more about the communication skills that you learned about in Part Two or if you'd like your parents to learn more about these skills, there are some excellent books available:

1. *Bringing Up Your Parents: The Adolescent's Handbook* by Alex J. Packer (Washington, D.C.: Acropolis Books, 1985). Most books on communication are written for parents to teach them how to avoid fights and solve problems with their kids. This is one of the few books that teaches kids these kinds of communication skills, and it is a truly terrific book!

For one thing, it's very, very funny, so you'll get a lot of laughs—but this book will do more than make you laugh. It'll teach you how to get along with your parents, or as the title indicates, it'll teach you how to "bring up" your parents.

2. *How To Talk So Kids Will Listen and Listen So Kids Will Talk* by Adele Faber and Elaine Mazlish (New York: Avon Books, 1982). This book was written for parents to help them learn how to communicate with their kids. It shows parents how to use skills like reflective listening and I-messages (although the

authors don't use quite these same words). It also teaches parents other ways of communicating that can help families. It's the kind of book that all kids wish their parents would read. It's a great book to give your parents for a present and it's easy enough to read that you'd probably enjoy it too. We highly recommend it for both parents and kids.

3. *P.E.T.: Parent Effectiveness Training* by Dr. Thomas Gordon (New York: New American Library, 1975). This is another great book, one that every parent should read. It teaches parents communication skills such as active listening and I/You-messages. Lynda first read Dr. Gordon's book when Area was just a toddler. We put Dr. Gordon's ideas to work in our family and we're delighted with the results. This is a great book to give your parent for mother's day or father's day. Or, borrow a copy from the library. In any case, get your parents to read this book. You'll be glad you did!

2: GETTING THE HELP YOU MAY NEED

If you are having problems with your parents (or in any area of your life, for that matter), you may need more help than this book, or any book, can give you. There are several ways to go about getting the help you may need.

• *Talking things over with a relative or family friend.* If you're having problems, one of the first steps is to find someone to talk to about them. If your problem is with one of your parents, can you talk it over with your other parent? Do you have an older brother or sister, an aunt or an uncle, a grandparent, or another relative or a friend who you could talk to?

The person you talk to may not be able to solve your problems, but simply having someone to talk to can be a big relief. Carrying your problems around inside you just isn't healthy.

• *Talking things over with someone outside your family or circle of friends.* Sometimes it's better to talk out your problems with someone who isn't so close as a relative or a friend. Does your school have a counselor? Is there a teacher you could talk to? If you belong to a church or temple (or even if you aren't a member), you might want to talk to the minister, the rabbi, or the priest. Many religious organizations have a youth director who is usually someone who has a great deal of experience working with young people and their problems.

It might seem difficult to approach someone you may not know all that well, but teachers, counselors, and youth directors, as well as ministers, rabbis, and priests, are used to having people approach them for help. That's part of their job. We think you'll find that these people will be very open to talking with you. And, because they have so much experience in dealing with problems, they'll be able to help you solve yours.

   • *Getting professional help.* Psychologists, psychiatrists, social workers, and counselors are all trained to deal with family conflicts and with other problems that teenagers face. They *can* and *do* help people to solve their problems.

Some people think that seeing a psychologist, a psychiatrist, or some other type of mental health professional means you're crazy. This simply isn't true. Perfectly sane and normal people have problems that they need professional help in solving. One boy who wrote to us put it very well when he said, "If you need help and don't go and get it, that's what's really crazy!"

Many boys and girls who've read our books have written to us about their problems. In some cases, we've suggested that they get professional help. So far, each and every kid we've suggested this to has written back to thank us. They've gone and gotten help, and their lives are much better for it. So, if you think you may need professional help, please get it. You owe it to yourself. You really do!

HOW TO GET PROFESSIONAL HELP

There are several ways to go about finding professional help. One way is to explain to your parents that you think you need professional help. If for some reason, you can't ask your parents, there are also other ways to get help.

If you're worried about how you'll pay for the help you need, please don't let this stop you. Some agencies provide free or very low-cost care. The psychologist, the psychiatrist, or the other mental health professional you see can help you figure out how to deal with the costs. The important thing is that you get help. You can figure out how to pay for the costs (if any) once you've found the person to help you.

If you decide you need professional help in dealing with your problems, the following are good places to look for it.

   • *Your school guidance counselor, a teacher, or a youth director at your church or temple.* These people will be able to refer you to a psychologist, a psychiatrist, or some other type of mental health professional. They can help you make an appointment and find a place where you can get help for free or at a price you can afford.

   • *Your doctor.* If you have a family doctor, he or she might be a good person to ask. Your doctor can help you find a clinic or community mental health group.

   • *Mental health clinics.* Look in the Yellow Pages under "Mental Health Clinics" or "Mental Health Services." Most local mental health clinics have special services for teenagers, and many will give you a free initial appointment (called an intake appointment or interview) to assess your problems and help you decide what kind of help you need. At some of these clinics, counseling for teens is free of charge, even after the first appointment.

• *Free clinics.* If there is a free clinic in your area, it may provide mental as well as physical health-care services. You can call or stop by.

• *Hot lines.* You can call the Information operator or the regular "O" operator and ask if there is a community hot line in your area. The people who answer the hot line phones can give you the numbers of free clinics, mental health clinics, and other community organizations that provide counseling for preteens and teens.

• *County department of public social services*: This number will be listed in your phone book under the name of your county, or you can get the number from the Information operator. Call them and ask to speak with a social worker. You can explain that you're a teen with some problems and you'd like to get some professional help. The social worker will help you get in touch with someone who can give you the help you need.

• *United Way information and referral services.* Most large cities have a United Way, which will be listed in the white pages. Call and ask for their information and referral number. Tell them that you're having problems and ask them to refer you to a group or organization that can help you.

• *Local radio stations.* Radio stations that broadcast mostly to teens often have lists of teen services in their communities. You can call and ask to speak to the public information director. If the station has a call-in show that deals with teens or with mental health, that's the best number to call. You don't have to go on the air or give your name, but you can ask them for a referral to a group in the community that can help you find counseling.

GETTING HELP FOR SPECIAL PROBLEMS

Some parents and/or kids have special problems that need professional help. For instance, some kids come from families where there is alcohol or drug abuse. Some kids are victims of physical or sexual abuse. Some kids are troubled by thoughts of suicide. Some kids have such serious problems that they've run away from home.

If you come from a family where there are these serious sorts of problems, you *definitely* need professional help. There's just no way a kid can handle these sorts of problems by himself or herself. You can get help by doing any of the kinds of things we've suggested above.

Since these special problems are such serious ones, we'd also like to talk a bit about each of them and mention some additional ways of getting help.

Runaways. If you have run away from home and feel lost and alone, there *is* help. You can get help by calling one of these numbers. Someone will help you.

You don't have to give your name or tell where you are unless you want to. They won't hassle you; they're there to help.

Runaway Hot Line. From all states except Texas, Alaska, and Hawaii, call 1-800-231-6946. From Texas, the number to call is 1-800-392-3352. These are toll-free numbers, so you don't have to pay for the call. These people can help you find a place to stay. If you want, they will call your family and relay the message that you are safe, without letting your parents know where you are.

National Runaway Switchboard. Call 1-800-621-4000. This, too, is a toll-free number, so you don't have to pay for the call. These people can also help you find a place to stay. If you want them to, they'll call your family to relay the message that you're safe. They won't tell your family where you are.

Suicide. If your problems with your parents or in some other area of your life are so serious that you've thought seriously about suicide, then you definitely need professional help. The above section, "How to Get Professional Help," will tell you how to go about getting this kind of help. Most cities also have suicide prevention hot lines that you can call twenty-four hours a day. Their number will be listed in the phone book under "Suicide" or "Suicide Prevention." In some parts of the country, the suicide hot line is run by a group called HELP or one called the Samaritans, so you might want to look under HELP or Samaritans in your phone book. You can also call the Information operator and ask for the number of a suicide prevention, crisis intervention, HELP, or Samaritan hot line. If the line is busy, keep calling. There are people out there who can help you!

Physical Abuse. It's sad to say, but the fact of the matter is that some kids who are physically abused don't even realize that what's happening to them is abnormal. They're so used to this kind of treatment that they think it's the normal or usual way for a parent to treat a child.

If you've ever had to go to a doctor or to an emergency room for medical treatment because of something your parent has done to you, you're a victim of physical abuse. If your parent has beaten you up or has left bruises or marks on your body, you're a victim of physical abuse. If your parent spanks you, this isn't necessarily physical abuse, but if your parent spanks you so hard, so long, or so often that you have bruises or marks, you are a victim of physical abuse. If your parent hits or slaps you in a moment of anger, this isn't necessarily physical abuse, but if this type of thing happens more routinely, you're a victim of physical abuse.

Don't make the mistake of thinking that there's something wrong with you, that you "had it coming" or that you deserve this kind of treatment. Sure, you may have done something wrong. Kids do. Your behavior or words may have provoked your parent, but no kid deserves to be physically abused, *no matter what.*

Normal parents have other ways of dealing with kids who misbehave. Normal parents don't physically abuse their kids.

If you are or think you are a victim of physical abuse, you need to get help. The parent who is abusing you is sick and needs help, too. Physical abuse doesn't usually stop or get better all by itself. In fact, it usually gets worse unless you get some help.

The first step toward getting help is to tell someone about what's happening. You can talk to a teacher; a school guidance counselor; a social worker; your priest, minister, or rabbi; or a mental health professional. You can call a hot line, a mental health clinic, or the police.

It may be difficult for you to take this first step of telling someone. Even though your parent is physically abusing you and you sometimes hate him or her for doing it, you may still also love your parent very much. You may be worried that, by telling, you'll get your parent into trouble. But the fact of the matter is that parents who abuse their children are *already* in trouble. Abusing parents have mental or emotional problems that are causing them to act the way they do. They need help and so do you. Neither you nor your parent can get the help you need unless you are willing to take the first step of telling someone.

If you need help and don't know where to turn, you can also write to us. Our address is at the end of Part One (page 72).

Sexual Abuse. Sexual abuse means that one person is pressuring or forcing another person to do sexual things that he or she doesn't want to do. The sexual things may be anything from touching, feeling, holding, caressing, kissing or licking the sexual organs, to actual sexual intercourse. When sexual abuse happens between family members, it is called incest.

Most victims of incest are girls who are victimized by a father, a stepfather, an uncle, an older brother, or some other male family member. Sometimes boys are victims of incest by a male relative, too. Incest between a boy or a girl and a female relative can and does happen, but it is very rare. Sometimes brothers and sisters engage in sex play with each other as they are growing up—playing "doctor" and so forth. This sort of thing isn't usually considered incest because both kids usually want to engage in this natural and normal sort of sex play and neither is being pressured or forced to do it. But if an older brother or sister pressures or forces a younger one to do sexual things, then it is considered incest.

Some incest victims feel the incest is their fault because they didn't fight back or somehow stop it from happening. But incest doesn't always involve force or violence as, for instance, rape does. Because of the older person's position in the family, he or she may be able to pressure a younger one into doing sexual things without actually having to use force. Some incest victims feel it's their fault because they may have enjoyed some aspect of the incest. Incest sometimes starts at a very early age, and only when a child gets older does she or he realize that these sexual activities are strange and just not normal.

Most incest victims feel a mixture of guilt, shame, humiliation, and anger. If you are a victim of incest, there's really only one thing to do: *Tell someone.* Telling someone can be *very, very* difficult. First of all, you may not be believed. If, for example, your mom won't believe you at first, try finding someone else, an aunt, a grandmother, an older sister, a teacher, or any adult who you feel *will* believe you. You can also call a local hotline or rape crisis center, Planned Parenthood, a woman's center, the YWCA, a community mental health center, or a mental health professional. It is important that you talk to someone. The Child Abuse National Hotline is toll free 1-800-422-4453. They provide a crisis intervention and referral center. You don't need to identify yourself, you can just talk. Their address is Post Office Box 630, Hollywood, Ca. 90028. If you don't feel you can do any of these things, you could write to us. Our address is on page 72.

Another thing that makes it difficult for some incest victims to tell someone is that they are worried that the person who has been abusing them will find out that they've told and will beat them up or hurt them or "take it out" on them in some way. If you are a victim of incest and aren't telling because you fear the abuser will get back at you, it's important for you to know that you *will* be protected. If you tell someone like a teacher, counselor, psychiatrist, psychologist, a hot-line person, a social worker, or the police, these people will arrange for your protection.

Yet another reason why incest victims find it difficult to tell someone is that they are afraid that telling will cause problems for the person who is abusing them or for the family as a whole. But the person who is abusing you *already* has a problem. People who commit incest are sick, but they can be cured. The person who commits incest needs help and so do you and, possibly, other family members as well. But, no one can get the help they need unless you take the first step of telling someone.

It's true that incest is a crime and that the person who has committed the incest can be sent to jail. (By the way, in case you don't know, victims of incest are *never* sent to jail; they are victims, not criminals.) Some incest victims don't tell because they don't want to see the person who's abusing them sent to jail. If this is the case with you, it's important for you to know that, in situations like yours, the judge doesn't usually send the abuser to jail. Instead, the judges send the abuser for psychiatric care so that person can be cured.

So, if you are a victim of incest, please, take that all-important first step of telling someone. If telling someone seems like something you just can't do, at least call the national hotline. You don't have to give your name, but at least you'll have someone to talk to about your problem.

Alcohol and Drug Abuse: If you or someone in your family is abusing drugs and/or alcohol, you need to get help. In addition to all the ways of getting help that we've already discussed there are special programs for people with drug and alcohol problems.

If you are the one who is abusing drugs or alcohol (or if you think you *might* have a drug or alcohol abuse problem), one of the best places for you to turn for help is Alcoholics Anonymous or Narcotics Anonymous. These organizations are support groups made up of people who have kicked their drug or alcohol problem, people who are trying to do so, and people who haven't yet kicked their habits, but would like to do so. These organizations have helped millions of people solve their drug and alcohol problems, and they can help you, too. There are local chapters of these organizations in almost every city and town in the country. In some areas, there's a twenty-four-hour hotline number you can call. In many parts of the country there are special teen chapters where teens help other teens overcome their problems. It doesn't cost anything to join. You only have to give your first name. There aren't any membership lists or forms to fill out, so no one, other than the other people in your chapter, has to know that you're part of these organizations unless you choose to tell them. To find out more about how these organizations can help you, look under "Alcoholics Anonymous" or "Narcotics Anonymous" in the white pages or call the Information operator and ask for the number of the chapter nearest you.

In addition to Alcoholics and Narcotics Anonymous, there are other programs and organizations that can help teens with drug or alcohol abuse problems. Look in the Yellow Pages under "Drug Abuse and Addiction Information and Treatment Centers" or under "Alcohol Abuse and Addiction Information and Treatment Centers." Call and explain your problem and ask how you can get help. If you can't find any listings in the Yellow Pages or if all the treatment programs sound too expensive, you can call your county department of social services. To find the right number, call the Information operator or look under your county, city, or state listings for the department of social services. Call the number and ask to speak to a social worker. Explain that you have a drug or alcohol problem and that you want help, and ask the social worker to recommend free or low-cost programs for teens in your area. It may take a few calls before you find the right person to talk to or the right program for you, but keep trying. There is help.

If, like many teens, you use alcohol or drugs, but aren't really sure that you actually have what could be considered a drug or alcohol abuse problem, we'd like to encourage you to call Alcoholics or Narcotics Anonymous or their hotline number. They can help you decide whether or not you have an abuse problem.

If one or both of your parents (or any family member, for that matter) is abusing drugs or alcohol, you and other family members may need help in dealing with the situation. Parents who have drug and alcohol abuse problems often behave in ways that make a happy family life difficult or even impossible.

Kids who grow up in families where the parents have alcohol or drug abuse problems react in many different ways. For instance, some kids knock themselves out trying to be the "perfect" kid. They hope that if they are "good" enough, the parent will stop drinking or taking drugs. Or, they hope that by being such a good kid, they'll be "proving" that there's really nothing wrong in their family. But, the hard truth is, no kid, no matter how great he or she is, can get a parent to stop drinking or taking drugs. Only the parents themselves can do that. Kids who try to solve their parents' drug or alcohol problems just end up wearing themselves out.

Sometimes parents who drink or take drugs will try to say that they are drinking or using drugs because of the way their kids are acting. Don't believe it!

If your parent or parents have a drug or alcohol abuse problem, you need help. You can't change the behavior of the person who's abusing the drugs or alcohol, but you can change the way you react to their problem. You can get help by following the suggestions already outlined, but perhaps the best way to get help is to call Alanon or Alateen. Like Alcoholics Anonymous and Narcotics Anonymous, Alanon and Alateen are support groups. But, Alanon and Alateen are for the family members and other relatives or people close to the drug and alcohol abusers. The people in these organizations understand what it's like to grow up in an alcohol or drug abusing family. They've helped millions of other people handle these problems and they can help you, too. You can find their number in the white pages under Alateen or Alanon or call the operator for the number. Call them, they can help!

About the Authors

Lynda Madaras is recognized worldwide by librarians, educators, reviewers, parents, nurses, and doctors—and kids, too—for her unique nonthreatening style, excellent organization, and thorough coverage of the emotional as well as physical experience of adolescence. A health educator and writer, she has been teaching sex education for over fifteen years and is the author of ten books including *Woman Care* and the bestsellers *The "What's Happening to My Body?" Book for Girls* and *The "What's Happening to My Body?" Book for Boys*. She lives in Los Angeles.

Area Madaras has collaborated with her mother on her books on adolescence since she was 13. She is now a graduate student at USC's Annenberg School of Communications.

Available from Newmarket Press

Lynda Madaras Books for Preteens and Teens (and their Families, Friends, and Teachers)

Lynda Madaras's growing-up books are highly recommended by reviewers, doctors, educators, librarians, and readers for their conversational tone ("Conversational, matter-of-fact, honest"—*Washington Post*) and coverage ("Madaras tackles some of the hardest subjects with the aim of provoking discussions rather than conveying her own point of view."—*Kirkus Reviews*).

The "What's Happening to My Body?" Book for Girls
A Growing-Up Guide for Parents and Daughters
Lynda Madaras with Area Madaras.
Foreword by Cynthia W. Cooke, M.D.
304 pages; 44 drawings; bibliography; index.

Selected as a "Best Book for Young Adults" by the American Library Association, this bestselling puberty education book provides detailed information about the body's changing size and shape, menstruation, breasts, changes in reproductive organs, and puberty in boys. Includes information appropriate for 8- to 15-year-olds on AIDS, STDs, and birth control.

The "What's Happening to My Body?" Book for Boys
A Growing-Up Guide for Parents and Sons
Lynda Madaras with Dane Saavedra.
Foreword by Ralph I. Lopez, M.D.
288 pages; 34 drawings; bibliography; index.

This acclaimed sequel to *The "What's Happening to My Body?" Book for Girls* provides answers to all the basic questions about the physical and emotional changes of male puberty. It includes a foreword for adults and chapters on the body's changing size and shape, hair, perspiration, pimples, voice changes, the reproductive organs, sexuality, and puberty in girls. Includes information appropriate for 8- to 15-year-olds on AIDS, STDs, and birth control.

Lynda Madaras Talks to Teen About AIDS
An Essential Guide for Parents, Teachers,
and Young People
Lynda Madaras. Foreword by Constance Wofsy, M.D.
128 pages; 9 drawings; resource guide; index.

Everything teens need to know to protect themselves against AIDS.
Written especially for 14- to 19-year-olds (whether sexually active or
not), this book separates the facts from the rumors, explains the
sexual transmission of AIDS and its prevention (including compre-
hensive information on abstinence and safe sex), and more.

My Body, My Self
The "What's Happening to My Body?"
Workbook for Girls
Lynda Madaras and Area Madaras
128 pages; 40 drawings.

With over 100 quizzes, checklists, and journal entries, this workbook
companion encourages girls to address head-on their questions and
concerns about their changing bodies. Everything affected by the
onset of puberty is covered from body image, diet, height, weight,
pimples, cramps, to first periods, first bras, and first impressions.

My Feelings, My Self
Lynda Madaras' Growing-Up Guide for Girls
Lynda Madaras with Area Madaras
160 pages; 30 drawings; bibliography; resource guide.

Focuses on relationships, feelings, self-knowledge, problem-solving
with parents, handling peer pressure, and making friends. Filled with
quizzes, exercises, letters, and information to help girls explore what
it feels like to be growing up.

Order from your local bookstore or write or call:
Newmarket Press, 18 East 48th Street, New York, NY 10017; (212) 832-3575

Please send me the following books by Lynda Madaras:

THE "WHAT'S HAPPENING TO MY BODY?" BOOK FOR GIRLS
_____ copies at $16.95 (gift hardcover)
_____ copies at $9.95 each (trade paperback)

THE "WHAT'S HAPPENING TO MY BODY?" BOOK FOR BOYS
_____ copies at $16.95 (gift hardcover)
_____ copies at $9.95 (trade paperback)

LYNDA MADARAS TALKS TO TEENS ABOUT AIDS
_____ copies at $16.95 each (gift hardcover)
_____ copies at $7.95 each (trade paperback)

MY BODY, MY SELF
_____ copies at $9.95 each (trade paperback)

MY FEELINGS, MY SELF
_____ copies at $9.95 each (trade paperback)

For postage and handling, add $2.00 for the first book, plus $1.00 for each additional book. Please allow 4-6 weeks for delivery.

I enclose a check or money order, payable to Newmarket Press, in the amount of $_____.

(NY residents please add sales tax.)

Name _____

Address _____

City/State/Zip _____

Organizations, clubs, firms, and other groups may qualify for special discounts on quantity purchases of these titles. For further information, or for a copy of our catalog, please contact the Special Sales Department, Newmarket Press, 18 East 48th Street, New York, NY 10017, or call (212) 832-3575.

Imbob.493